Kenmore Microwave Cooking

A Rutledge Book
The Benjamin Company, Inc.
New York, New York

Kenmore Microwave Cooking

Project Coordinator: Carol A. Hartman
Consulting Home Economist: Betty Sullivan
Project Director: Robert C. Dougherty
Associate Director: Susan Henkel

USER INSTRUCTIONS

PRECAUTIONS TO AVOID POSSIBLE EXPOSURE TO EXCESSIVE MICROWAVE ENERGY
(a) DO NOT ATTEMPT to operate this oven with the door open since open-door operation can result in harmful exposure to microwave energy. It is important not to defeat or tamper with the safety interlocks.
(b) DO NOT PLACE any object between the oven front face and the door or allow soil or cleaner residue to accumulate on sealing surfaces.
(c) DO NOT OPERATE the oven if it is damaged. It is particularly important that the oven door closes properly and that there is no damage to the:
    (1) DOOR (bent)
    (2) HINGES AND LATCHES (broken or loosened)
    (3) DOOR SEALS AND SEALING SURFACES
(d) THE OVEN SHOULD NOT BE ADJUSTED OR REPAIRED BY ANYONE EXCEPT PROPERLY QUALIFIED SERVICE PERSONNEL.

Copyright 1979 in all countries of the International Copyright Union by The Benjamin Company, Inc.

All rights reserved, including the right of reproduction in whole or in part.

Library of Congress Catalog Card Number: 78-71995
ISBN: 0-87502-064-X
Prepared and produced by Rutledge Books, Inc.
Published by The Benjamin Company, Inc.
485 Madison Avenue
New York, New York 10022
Printed in Japan
Fifth Printing 1979

Photographs by Walter Storck Studios, Inc.; photograph, page 35, by William Pell; illustrations by Tom Huffman

Contents

THE NO-NONSENSE BASICS

The microwave oven is fast becoming an essential appliance for every kitchen. But let's set something straight: the microwave oven, or microwaving as a cooking method, does not replace anything. It does not totally replace your conventional range. It does not totally replace your conventional oven. It most assuredly does not replace you, the cook, and your vital cooking instincts.

Yes, the distinctive difference in microwave cooking is its incredible speed. But if you're to be a successful microwave cook, your first virtue must be patience. It's natural to want to rush to the recipes and start cooking. Please, relax first in your favorite chair and read these essential introductory chapters.

HOW DOES IT WORK?

With conventional methods, food cooks by heat applied to the bottom of the pan or by hot air which surrounds the food. With the microwave oven, *microwaves* travel directly to the food. Somewhat like radio waves or television waves, they are generated by a magnetron tube. These waves pass right through microproof cookware (cookware recommended for microwave oven use). They do not heat the cookware. They do not heat the air, either. Of course, foods and liquids cooked for extended periods of time may transfer some of their heat to your microproof cookware and you will find an occasional use for hot pads. These waves do, however, bounce off oven sides, so the oven cannot be operated with the door open.

INSTALLATION AND MAINTENANCE

To install your oven, *follow manufacturer's directions carefully*. A microwave oven operates on standard 110-120v household current and does not require an expert to ready it for regular use.

Maintenance requires a few simple cleaning steps. Again, *follow your manufacturer's directions*. Since there is little splattering with microwave cooking, you'll find that the buildup of grease or the like is minimal; an occasional wiping is all that is required to keep the oven clean.

Keep the door and door gasket free of food buildup to maintain a tight seal.

TIMING AND YOUR INSTINCTS

Time is the most important factor in microwave cooking. But isn't that statement true for all cooking? You, the cook, have to be the judge, applying your family's preferences and your own instincts. Chances are, you can tell if a turkey is done simply by looking at it! You might even scoff at the timing chart given on the package because you know it always seems to need more or less time. However, perhaps because the microwave oven is a product of computer technology, we fail to acknowledge that it is no more precise than any other cooking method.

It's true that timing is more critical in microwave cooking than in conventional methods. It's hard to imagine one minute causing a significant difference in conventional cooking. It probably wouldn't make a difference with a turkey, roast or stew. But, even in conventional cooking, one minute can easily wreck a sauce, a pie shell, and can produce terribly overdone broiled foods.

So, when you consider that a cooking task requiring one hour conventionally may need only 4 to 4½ minutes by microwaving (a single baked potato, for example) you can understand why microwave cooking requires a bit different approach to timing. One minute is always significant in microwave cooking. As a result, most microwave recipes express probable minimum-maximum cooking times, as in "Cook on 70 (roast) for 4 to 5 minutes."

Why can't cooking times be precise? If a way could be found to guarantee that our foods would be exactly the same each time we cook them, you could come close to precise cooking times. Then the utility would have to guarantee not to alter our source of power (there are frequent changes in the voltage levels reaching our homes). The fact simply is that one potato varies from another in density, moisture content, shape, weight, and temperature. The same is true for all foods. If it sounds complicated, all it really comes down to is a confirmation of the fact that you, not the microwave oven, are the cook. The oven can't make decisions, so you must.

FOODS THAT DO WELL AND SOME THAT DON'T

There are many foods which cook so well in a microwave oven that you'll soon not even think of cooking them any other way. Casseroles, appetizers, candies, vegetables, baked potatoes, fish, bacon, most cakes — many things are noticeably better. Roasts, pies, puddings — just about everything else is at least as good as when cooked by conventional methods. Processes such as softening or melting ingredients in their wrapper, defrosting (remove foods from metal pans), blanching in preparation for freezing — all give superb results.

The microwave oven does not do the following products well and should not be used for cooking: eggs in the shell; deep fat frying; home canning; toasting or anything calling for crust development; Angel Food Cake; popovers; popcorn; and, certain dishes which owe their characteristic flavor to a long cooking process.

Microwave popcorn popping devices are available. While safe to use, they usually do not give results equal to conventional popping methods. If used, carefully follow the instructions provided with the popping product.

ADAPTING YOUR OWN RECIPES

One of the most frequently asked questions is whether or not your favorite conventional recipes can be used. Yes, they can, and that's the true measure of an accomplished microwave cook. It takes some ingenuity and experimentation on your part but it is fun to do and you'll be quite proud to pass on your accomplishments to friends. The techniques for adapting your recipes to the microwave method are not very sophisticated.

First, find a recipe in this book similar to the recipe you'd like to adapt. The recipe chapters give some hints on adapting. Use those hints and follow the cooking time, microproof container size, and power setting from the microwave recipe you've selected as being most like the conventional recipe you'd like to use. If no similar microwave recipe can be found, cook for 20-25% of conventional cooking time at the setting which seems best to you. Consider it something of an experiment, though, and adjust for better results next time. Soon your microwave talent will develop to the point where you'll no longer need to hunt for a comparable microwave recipe!

TERMS AND PROCEDURES YOU NEED TO KNOW

In general, microwave cooking uses the same terms as conventional cooking. However, because the oven works so quickly, some terms become more vital. There are also unique procedures. Familiarity with these terms and procedures will help you become a skilled microwave cook more quickly.

ARRANGEMENT

If there are several pieces of similar foods, arrange them in a circular fashion. Potatoes in a ring; corn on the cob like the spokes of a wheel (from the oven's center out to the sides). Chicken pieces, chops, and other meats with bones should be placed so that the bony parts face the center, the thick parts face the outside. Similarly, in reheating a plate of leftovers, denser foods are placed toward the outer edge. More porous foods like rolls or fluffy rice can be placed in the center of the plate.

BOTTOM SHELF

Your oven is equipped with a removable middle rack. When in use, the rack has the appearance of a middle shelf. The bottom oven shelf is the primary cooking level. Unless otherwise noted, all microwave cooking is done on the bottom oven shelf.

BROWNING

After ten minutes or so, meats and poultry brown. A special microwave browning dish or grill is available for meats (hamburgers, chops, steak) that cook too quickly for browning. You can also create a browned look by brushing on a gravy mix or bottled brown bouquet. Cakes, breads, and pie shells don't brown well. That isn't important with chocolate or spice cakes, for example. For others, molasses or dark syrups may be brushed on, or glazes and frostings used.

CONTAINER SELECTION

If a particular size or shape of microproof cooking container is specified in a recipe, it should be used. Varying container size or shape may vary cooking time. Generally, a tall, narrow container increases cooking time; a broad, shallow container reduces cooking time. Recipes for puddings and sauces call for large containers to prevent boilovers. Cakes and some loaf recipes call for round cookware to provide more even cooking.

COVERINGS

Covers trap steam, speeding cooking time and helping foods retain their natural moisture. Suitable coverings are microproof casserole tops, glass covers, plastic wrap, waxed paper, microproof plates and saucers. Paper toweling is also very useful as a covering to prevent splatters but it does not trap steam. Remove coverings away from hands and face to prevent steam burns.

DELICATE INGREDIENTS

Foods such as mayonnaise, cheese, eggs, milk, cream, and dairy sour cream require lower settings for proper cooking. They may toughen, separate, or curdle at higher settings. Low settings are also used for mushrooms and kidney beans because higher settings may cause them to "pop."

DENSITY

A meat roast has a high density. Baked breads have low density. Simply, there is little air in foods of high density. It takes much longer for a slice of meat to reheat than for slice of bread, even though they may be a similar size.

MEAL PLANNING

Use of the oven rack and bottom shelf enables you to have several foods cooking simultaneously. Generally, you'll put foods that need to cook the longest in first and add others later. Another meal planning method is to prepare desserts early; cook meat, such as a roast; and, cook vegetables during the Standing Time for the

7

meat. One-dish meals are fine, too, topped off with warmed rolls, a salad, and a dessert that cooks while you eat the main course.

MICROPROOF

A term presented for the first time in this cookbook. It's used to refer to cookware or utensils that are safe and recommended for microwave cooking. Glass is always safe, so the term is not used when glass is specified. See details in the Microproof Cookware chapter.

MOISTURE

Just-picked vegetables contain much more moisture than those that were picked weeks or months ago (such as potatoes). The more moisture in the food, the less dense it is likely to be, so it will need less cooking time.

MULTI-POWER

Your microwave oven gives you the ability to select from many power settings. You can adjust your multi-power oven to suit food being cooked or to achieve a desired method. Many microwave ovens offer only one setting.

PROGRAMMING

Your microwave oven does have a built-in computer. The computer accepts your instructions, your "programming," and causes the oven to perform accordingly.

RACK

The removable middle "shelf" of your oven. Used primarily in Whole Meal cooking methods.

ROTATING

For uniform cooking results, certain foods (pies, mostly) are rotated one-quarter turn one or more times during the cooking process. This provides especially even distribution of the microwave energy.

STANDING TIME

The standing times specified in the recipes and in the charts are really a part of the cooking times. Food continues to cook after it is removed from the oven. Food of higher density requires a longer standing time. For meats, standing time also helps retain natural juices and makes carving easier.

STARTING TEMPERATURE

Unless otherwise noted, recipes anticipate that ingredients will be added at their customary storage temperatures. So, if canned peas are called for and you substitute frozen, the cooking time will be a bit longer. Milk is usually added direct from the refrigerator; if you use milk at room temperature, for some reason, the cooking time will be a bit less.

STIRRING

Because microwaves cook the outside of foods first, the center portion sometimes needs redistribution for even cooking. When a recipe directs, always stir from the outside in, so that heat is equalized and uncooked portions flow toward the outside edges.

TEMPERATURE PROBE

A special feature of your oven, the temperature probe enables you to cook food without setting times. With the temperature probe properly inserted and programmed, the oven automatically cooks the food to the preselected temperature.

TURNING

In the case of large, dense foods such as roasts, turning the food over will help to cook it evenly.

VOLUME

If you are baking several potatoes for example, the cooking time will be longer than if you were baking just one. Three cups of water take longer to heat than just one cup. As a guide, if you halve a recipe cook the food a little longer than half the full-recipe time. Then check at short intervals, until the food is cooked to your taste.

MICROPROOF COOKWARE

There is such a wide variety of cookware and cooking implements that are acceptable for microwave use that we've given them all a new name, MICROPROOF. In short, a microproof item is any cooking utensil made of a material which is safe for microwave use. Except as specifically directed, items made of metal, even partially, are never to be used in the microwave oven. Most other materials are microproof for at least limited microwave cooking use.

Check manufacturer's directions. Check the Microproof Cookware chart. Review the Materials Checklist. If still in doubt, place 1 cup of water in a glass measure on the container or dish to be tested. Place in the oven and cook on HI (max. power) for 1 minute. If the dish feels hot, *don't use it*. If it feels warm, the dish may be used only for warming food. If it remains at room temperature, it is MICROPROOF.

The rapid growth of microwave cooking has, fortunately, created many new products for microwave cooking use. Chief among these are microproof replacements for favorite cookware previously available only in metal. You'll find a wide variety at your store: cake pans, bundt-type molds, bacon racks, roasting racks, etc. When you add those to microproof traditional cookware and the incredible array of paper products which can be used, you find that microwave cooking enables you to select from more kinds of cookware than available for conventional cooking.

MATERIALS CHECKLIST

- PLASTICS: May be used if dishwasher safe, but only for limited cooking periods or for heating. Do not use plastics for tomato-based foods or foods with high fat or high sugar contents.
- PLASTIC COOKING POUCHES: Can be used if metal twist ties are removed. Substitute string, if necessary. Slit pouch so steam can escape.
- PAPER: Approved for short-term cooking and for reheating at low settings. Must not be foil-lined. Extended use may cause it to burn. Waxed paper is also suitable for coverings.
- STRAW AND WOOD: Can be used for quick warming. Be certain no metal is used in fastening straw or wood items.
- METALS: Not suitable because they reflect microwaves preventing effective cooking. Also, metal touching oven sides can cause sparks.
- APPROVED METAL USES: On large pieces of meat or poultry, *small strips of aluminum foil* can be used to cover areas (wing tips, breast bone, etc.) that defrost or cook more rapidly than the rest of the piece. TV dinners with foil covers removed can be heated in their *shallow aluminum trays* provided that the trays do not exceed ¾" in depth. Trays or any foil item must be at least 1" from oven walls. (However, TV dinners heat much faster if you "pop" the blocks of food out and arrange them on microproof dinner plates.)
- CHINA, POTTERY: Ideal for microwave use. However, if they have metallic trim or glaze they are not microproof and should not be used.
- GLASS: An excellent microwave cooking material. Especially useful for baking, to check doneness through the bottom. Since glass is always safe, "microproof" is not used when a glass item is specified.
- THERMOMETERS: Your temperature probe is all you need, except as directed in specific recipes. If you wish to use a meat thermometer, only approved microwave oven meat thermometers may be used.

MICROPROOF COOKWARE

Item	Good Use	General Notes
China plates, cups (no metal trim)	Heating dinners and drinks.	
Pottery plates, mugs, and bowls	Heating dinners, soups, drinks.	Some pottery has a metallic glaze. To check, use dish test.
Earthenware plates, mugs, etc.	Heating dinners, soups, drinks.	Also known as "ironstone." See pottery (above) for glaze data.
Corelle® Livingware	Heating dinners, soups, drinks.	Closed-handle cups should not be used.
Paper plates, cups, napkins	Heating hot dogs, drinks, rolls.	Absorb moisture from baked goods and freshen them.
Soft plastics, sherbet cartons	Reheating leftovers.	Used for short reheating periods. Do not use to reheat acid-based foods or those with high fat or sugar content.
Corning Ware® casseroles	Cooking main dishes, vegetables, desserts.	
Pyrex® casseroles	Cooking main dishes, vegetables, desserts.	Do not use dishes with metal trim, as sparks may occur.
TV dinner trays (metal)	Frozen dinners or homemade dinners.	No deeper than ¾". Food will receive heat from the top surface only.
Oven film and cooking bags	Cooking roasts or stews.	Substitute string for metal twist ties. Bag itself will not cause tenderizing. Do not use film with foil edges.
Cooking pouches	Cooking meats, vegetables, rice, other frozen foods.	Slit pouch so steam can escape.
Waxed paper	Wrapping corn on the cob; covering casseroles.	Food temperature may cause some melting. (Wax will not adhere to hot food.)
Plastic wrap	Covering dishes.	Puncture to allow steam to escape.
Wooden spoons	Stirring puddings and sauces.	Can withstand microwaves for short cooking periods.
Microwave roasting racks	Cooking roasts and chickens.	
Microwave browning dishes or grills	Searing, grilling, and frying small meat items; grilling sandwiches.	These utensils are specially made to absorb microwaves and to preheat to high temperatures. They brown pieces of meat that otherwise would not brown in a microwave oven.

Many kinds of dishes—but nothing metal—can be used in the microwave oven.

LET'S USE THE OVEN

Now, for some practical experience, let's melt a bit of butter. Put 1 tablespoon butter or margarine in a 1-cup glass measure. Place in oven; close oven door. Touch "Clear" pad. Touch "Time" pad; then touch 3; touch 0. Time is now set for 30 seconds. Now, touch the "Cook Control" pad; touch 7; touch 0. The oven is now programmed to cook on 70 (roast) for ½ minute. Touch "Start". Observe. After 30 seconds, butter should be melted. Keep in mind that the temperature of the butter when you began, and other factors, change results. If you note that the butter was melted after 20 seconds, you'll know to adjust next time. If it is not melted after 30 seconds, reset oven for 10 seconds and observe.

As you become accustomed to working with your oven, you may like more flexibility in determining settings. For example, perhaps you want a setting between 70 (roast) and 80 (reheat). Set the time as usual, touch the "Cook Control" pad, then touch 7 and 5. The Display Window will show "75", indicating that your oven is set to operate at a 75% power level. You can control results so that the end product suits your taste.

On the front of your oven, you'll find a control panel listing the ten settings which appear in the chart below. They refer to percentages of microwave power from 10% to 100% and to familiar cooking processes and techniques. Study the chart.

COOKING GUIDE FOR MULTI-POWER SETTINGS

Setting	Typical Uses
10 (warm)	Softening cream cheese; raising bread dough; keeping casseroles and main dishes warm.
20 (low)	Softening chocolate; heating breads, rolls, pancakes, and French toast. Clarifying butter; taking chill off fruit; heating small amounts; tacos and tortillas.
30 (defrost)	Thawing meats, poultry, and seafood. Cooking pasta. Finish cooking casseroles, stews, and some sauces.
40 (braise)	Cooking less tender cuts of meat in liquid and slow cooking dishes. Finish cooking less tender roasts. Cooking baked custards.
50 (simmer)	Cooking sauces, stews, and soups.
60 (bake)	Starting muffins and quick breads. (Finish on HI.)
70 (roast)	Cooking rump roasts, ham, veal, and lamb; cooking cheese dishes; defrosting large cuts of meat and poultry. Cooking eggs and meat loaves.
80 (reheat)	Quickly reheating precooked or prepared foods.
90 (saute)	Quickly cooking onions, celery, green peppers. Reheating meat slices quickly.
HI (max. power)	Cooking tender cuts of meat. Cooking poultry, fish, vegetables, and most casseroles; preheating the browning dish.

THE TEMPERATURE PROBE

Your microwave oven has a unique feature, available only on the most sophisticated models. Cooking with the temperature probe does not require time calculations. Preferred and accurate internal temperatures of foods at various levels of doneness have been established for many years. The temperature probe automatically senses the temperature of the food.

This feature offers a number of advantages. You do not have to select the amount of cooking time. You can see food temperature in the Display Window. If you have serving delays, don't worry. The oven has an automatic "hold warm" feature. The temperature probe controls the oven, maintains the correct food temperature.

"Guide to the Temperature Probe" provides a range from 120° to 175°, the food temperatures generally used. (The temperature probe does not provide control for very high food temperatures, such as those necessary for many candy recipes.)

GUIDE TO THE TEMPERATURE PROBE

Temperature Probe Settings

120° Fully Cooked Ham
125° Rare Beef
135° Medium Beef
140° Meat Loaf
150° Reheat Casseroles
155° Well Done Beef, Pork, Veal
160° Reheat Vegetables
165° Well Done Lamb
170° Reheat Beverages
175° Reheat Potatoes

Tips for Probe Use
1. Place food in container, as recipe directs.
2. Plug temperature probe into the side of oven cavity.
3. Place temperature probe in food, as recipe directs. A horizontal position, or as close to horizontal as possible is best.

4. Make sure the larger end of the temperature probe, inserted in the food, does not touch the food, cooking container, or the sides of the oven.
5. Touch "Clear".
6. Touch "Temperature Control". Select temperature.
7. If a power setting other than HI (max. power) is desired, touch "Cook Control". Set power level.
8. Touch "Start".
9. Never operate oven with temperature probe in cavity unless probe is plugged in and inserted in food.
10. Use hot pads to remove temperature probe. It may be hot.

THE DEFROSTING SPECIALTY

One of the nicest special functions of your microwave oven is defrosting. The 30 (defrost) setting is used for most foods. Some exceptions are provided in the recipe-chapter charts. A few tips:

• Some large food items require more standing time than others.
• Poultry wings, legs, and small or bony ends of meat might need to be covered with aluminum foil strips for most of the thawing-time to prevent cooking.
• Large items should be turned and rotated halfway through defrosting time to provide more even thawing.
• Foods in approved coverings thaw more quickly.
• Remove thawed portions of ground meat as soon as thawed, returning frozen portions to the oven.
• To thaw half of a frozen vegetable package, wrap half the package with aluminum foil. When unwrapped side is thawed, separate that portion; return balance to freezer.
• Thin or sliced items should be separated as soon as possible; remove thawed pieces and allow others to continue thawing.

APPETIZERS

Parties will be more fun and much easier for you with the help of your microwave oven. Those last-minute hassles are gone. You can prepare award-winning canapes ahead and heat them in minutes, or moments, as needed! It's a sure bet that you'll soon rate among the most accomplished hosts or hostesses. While this chapter presents many recipes for entertaining, you'll also find many TV-side nibbles and munchies for the family.

ADAPTING YOUR OWN RECIPES

Adapting your conventional recipes for ap-

petizers to microwave cooking will generally be quite easy to do. Most dips, toppings, and finger foods tend to have similar densities. Thus, for example, the timing and method for 2 cups of your favorite dip will be rather close to the recipes here. Some tips for adapting recipes and serving appetizers:

- Toppings for canapés can be made ahead, but should be placed on bread or crackers just before heating to assure crisp canapé bases. Toasted bread works best.
- Use paper toweling or paper napkins as underliners when heating canapés, egg rolls, etc. It helps absorb moisture and prevents sogginess. Discard paper after heating and place food on serving tray.
- Heating time depends on the amount and type of appetizer.
- Cheese dips and similar mixtures retain their heat longer when prepared in a microwave oven. They should be stirred once during the cooking time and upon completion.
- Appetizers with sour cream, mayonnaise, salad dressing, eggs, and dairy products as major ingredients are heated at lower power settings to avoid separating.

Cocktail Wieners

24 wieners

¼ cup minced onion	2 tablespoons brown sugar
2 teaspoons butter	½ teaspoon salt
½ cup catsup	½ teaspoon dry mustard
1 tablespoon vinegar	½ teaspoon paprika
½ teaspoon Worcestershire sauce	2 dozen cocktail wieners

1. Combine onion and butter in a 1- to 1½-quart microproof casserole. Cover and cook on 90 (saute) for 3 minutes, or until onion is transparent.
2. Add ¼ cup water and stir in remaining ingredients except cocktail wieners. Cover and cook on HI (max. power) for 2½ minutes, or until sauce is bubbly.
3. Stir in cocktail wieners. Cover and cook on HI (max. power) for 4 minutes, or until wieners are hot.
4. Let stand, covered, for 2 minutes.
5. Serve warm; use toothpicks to spear individual wieners.

Cocktail Wieners (recipe above); Bean Dip, Hot Mexican Cheese Dip (recipes, p. 16)

Bean Dip *(Illustrated on page 15)* 3 cups

1 can (16 ounces) baked or kidney
  beans
1 jar (8 ounces) pasteurized process
  cheese spread

¼ cup chili sauce
1 teaspoon chili powder
  Dash hot-pepper sauce

1. Pour beans into a 1½-quart microproof casserole. Mash beans with a fork. Add remaining ingredients and blend well. Cover and cook on 60 (bake) for 2 to 3 minutes. Stir well.
2. Cover and cook on 50 (simmer) for 2 to 3 minutes, or until hot.
3. Keep hot on a heated tray or a candle warmer. Serve with corn chips.

Hot Mexican Cheese Dip 2½ cups
(Illustrated on page 15)

1 pound process American cheese,
  grated

1 can (10 ounces) green chilies and
  tomatoes

1. Combine cheese and chilies in a 1½-quart microproof casserole. Cover and cook on 80 (reheat) for 5 minutes. Mix thoroughly with portable mixer until smooth.
2. Keep hot on a heated tray or candle warmer, and serve with corn chips or potato chips or with crisp raw vegetables.

Sweet and Sour Hot Dogs 40 pieces

2 tablespoons prepared mustard
¼ cup grape jelly

½ pound frankfurters
1 teaspoon butter or margarine, melted

1. Combine mustard and jelly in a 1-cup glass measure. Cover with plastic wrap and cook on 60 (bake) for 3 minutes.
2. Cut each frankfurter diagonally in 8 slices. Place butter and frankfurters in 1-quart microproof casserole. Cover and cook on HI (max. power) for 2 minutes.
3. Pour grape jelly sauce over frankfurters. Cover and cook on HI (max. power) for 4 minutes. Let stand 2 minutes.
4. Serve hot; use toothpicks to spear individual slices.

Lemon Chicken Wings

28 pieces

3 pounds chicken wings
½ cup salad oil
½ cup lemon juice

1 clove garlic, crushed
1 teaspoon salt
½ teaspoon pepper

1. Cut chicken wings apart at both joints, discard tips. Combine remaining ingredients in 12- x 7-inch microproof baking dish. Add chicken pieces and let stand about 1 hour, turning chicken pieces several times.
2. Cover with waxed paper and cook on HI (max. power) for 6 minutes.
3. Turn chicken pieces over and cook on HI (max. power) for 6 to 7 minutes or until chicken is tender. Remove garlic clove.
4. Let stand, covered, 5 minutes before serving.

Your guests will be delighted if you serve these as finger food at your next cocktail party. You might provide extra napkins as a courtesy.

Cheddar Cheese Canapés

24 canapés

¼ cup grated Cheddar cheese
2 tablespoons light cream
1 tablespoon grated Parmesan cheese
⅛ teaspoon Worcestershire sauce

⅛ teaspoon hot-pepper sauce
1 tablespoon sesame seeds
24 rounds of toast or crisp crackers
Chopped parsley

1. Combine Cheddar cheese, cream, Parmesan cheese, Worcestershire, hot-pepper sauce, and sesame seeds. Blend with an electric mixer until smooth. Spread 1 teaspoon of the mixture on each of the toast rounds or crackers.
2. Arrange 12 canapés on a microproof platter lined with paper towels. Cook on 70 (roast) for 20 to 30 seconds, or until mixture is warm and cheese is melted. Repeat with remaining·canapés.
3. Garnish with parsley; serve warm.

Crab Supremes

16 to 18 canapés

1 can (6½ to 7 ounces) crabmeat
½ cup finely minced celery
2 teaspoons prepared mustard
4 teaspoons chopped sweet pickle relish

½ cup mayonnaise
Crisp crackers or toast rounds

1. Drain crabmeat. Place in a 1-quart bowl and flake with a fork. Add celery, mustard, pickle relish, and mayonnaise. Mix well. Spread mixture on crackers or toast rounds. Place 8 at a time on a microproof plate lined with a paper towel. Cover with waxed paper.
2. Cook on 70 (roast) for 30 to 45 seconds, or until hot. Repeat with remaining canapés.

Meatball Appetizers

about 60

1 pound lean ground beef
½ pound ground pork
1 small onion, finely minced
1 cup milk
1 egg, lightly beaten

1 cup dry bread crumbs
1 teaspoon salt
¼ teaspoon pepper
¼ teaspoon ground allspice

1. Combine ingredients in a large mixing bowl and blend well. Form into small balls, about 1 inch in diameter.
2. Arrange half of the meatballs in a single layer in an oblong microproof baking dish. Cook, uncovered, on 60 (bake) for 4 minutes.
3. Place in a chafing dish to keep hot.
4. Cook remaining meatballs and add to chafing dish. Serve hot. Use toothpicks to spear meatballs, dunk in Hot Savory Dip (below).

Hot Savory Dip

2 cups

1 can (6 ounces) evaporated milk
1 cup shredded sharp Cheddar cheese
1 cup shredded Swiss cheese

1 tablespoon prepared mustard
1 teaspoon Worcestershire sauce
Dash hot-pepper sauce

1. Put all ingredients in a 1½-quart microproof casserole. Cover and cook on 60 (bake) for 6 minutes. Stir thoroughly halfway through cooking time.
2. Serve as a warm dip for meatballs and/or vegetables. Keep warm on stand over a lighted candle or fondue burner.

This is also great as a sauce for cooked cauliflower or other vegetables. Leftover dip can simply be rewarmed and poured over vegetables at serving time.

Shrimp Dip

2 cups

1 can (10½ ounces) cream of shrimp soup, undiluted
1 package (8 ounces) cream cheese, softened

1 teaspoon lemon juice
Dash paprika
Dash garlic powder

1. Pour soup into a small microproof mixing bowl. Cover with waxed paper and cook on 60 (bake) for 3 minutes, or until hot. Stir well.
2. Beat in cream cheese, lemon juice, paprika, and garlic powder. Cook on 60 (bake) for 1½ to 2 minutes, or until hot.
3. Serve as a dip with crisp vegetables or shrimp.

Shrimp Dip disappears quickly, but if your guests are late or tend to dawdle, keep sauce hot with a candle warmer.

*Meatball Appetizers, Hot Savory Dip, Shrimp Dip
(recipes, above); Cocktail Shrimp (recipe, p. 20)*

Cocktail Shrimp *(Illustrated on page 18)* about 36

1 pound medium-sized raw shrimp

1. Arrange shrimp in single layer on flat, round microproof plate with shrimp tails toward the center. Cover with waxed paper and cook on 70 (roast) for 5 to 7 minutes, or until shrimp turn pink.
2. Let stand 4 minutes; then shell. Devein, if desired. Serve cold with Spicy Dipping Sauce (below) or Shrimp Dip (page 19).

Spicy Dipping Sauce 1¼ cups

1 can (10¾ ounces) cream of
  mushroom soup, undiluted
1½ tablespoons curry powder

1 clove garlic, minced
1 tablespoon lemon juice

1. Stir all ingredients together in a 4-cup glass measure until blended. Cook on HI (max. power) for 2 minutes or until hot.
2. Serve hot with either bite-size meatballs, cubed sirloin, shrimp, or scallops.

Rumaki about 36

12 slices bacon
 8 ounces chicken livers
¼ teaspoon garlic powder

¼ cup soy sauce
1 can (8 ounces) sliced water
  chestnuts, drained

1. Cut bacon slices in thirds and chicken livers in 1-inch pieces. Mix garlic powder in soy sauce.
2. Dip chicken livers in soy sauce. Place 1 slice of water chestnut in 1 piece of liver and wrap in 1 slice of bacon. Roll, secure and fasten with wooden toothpick. Place 10 at a time in a circle on a paper towel lined microproof plate; cover with a paper towel. Cook on HI (max. power) for 4 minutes.
3. Turn over, cover, and cook on HI (max. power) for 3 minutes, or until bacon is cooked.
4. Allow to stand 1 minute before serving.

You can be creative with Rumaki! Try such variations as whole stuffed olives, shrimp, or prunes substituted for chicken livers. Yes, prunes: they're delicious! Rumaki can also be cooked directly on a microwave roasting rack, covered with a paper towel.

Shrimp Olive Dip

about 2½ cups

1 can (10½ ounces) cream of shrimp
  soup, undiluted
1 package (8 ounces) cream cheese,
  cut into chunks
1 can (8 ounces) chopped ripe olives,
  drained

2 tablespoons lemon juice
1 teaspoon Worcestershire sauce
¾ teaspoon curry powder

1. Combine soup and cream cheese in a 1-quart microproof casserole. Cover and cook on 60 (bake) for 3 minutes.
2. Remove and stir until cheese is well blended. Stir in remaining ingredients. Cover and cook on 60 (bake) for 2 to 3 minutes, or until hot.
3. Place over a candle warmer to keep hot and serve as a dip with corn chips or potato chips.

If you like the sharpness but don't care for curry powder, substitute cayenne pepper.
For a milder dip, simply eliminate the curry powder.

Stuffed Mushrooms

about 50

1 pound small fresh mushrooms
4 slices bacon, diced
2 tablespoons minced green pepper
¼ cup minced onion
½ teaspoon salt

1 package (3 ounces) cream cheese
¼ teaspoon Worcestershire sauce
1 tablespoon butter or margarine
½ cup soft bread crumbs

1. Wash and dry mushrooms, remove stems. Chop stems, set aside.
2. Combine bacon, green pepper, and onion in a 4-cup glass measure. Cover with paper towel and cook on HI (max. power) for 4 minutes, stirring once. Drain fat.
3. Add salt, cream cheese, Worcestershire, and mushroom stems. Mix well. Fill mushrooms with bacon mixture.
4. Mix butter and bread crumbs in 2-cup glass measure. Cook on HI (max. power) for 1 minute. Press bread crumbs into top of bacon mixture. Place half of mushrooms on 9-inch square microproof baking dish, stuffing side up. Cook on HI (max. power) for 1 to 2 minutes. Repeat with remaining mushrooms.

Hot Beef Munchies

27 canapés

½ pound lean ground round steak
2 tablespoons minced onion
1 teaspoon catsup
½ teaspoon prepared mustard

½ teaspoon prepared horseradish sauce
27 melba toast rounds
Garlic salt

1. Combine meat, onion, catsup, mustard, and horseradish sauce. Blend well. Put about 1 teaspoon of the mixture on top of each toast round. Sprinkle with garlic salt.
2. Cook, uncovered, 9 at a time on a paper towel on HI (max. power) for 50 seconds, or to the desired degree of doneness. Remove to serving plate at once and serve.

Expecting an extra-large group? Then keep in mind that this recipe doubles well. For best results, top toast rounds immediately before cooking.

Nachoes

30 canapés

1 can (3⅛ ounces) jalapeño bean dip
1 can (5¼ ounces) tortilla chips

1½ cups grated Cheddar cheese
1 can (2¼ ounces) sliced

1. Spread bean dip lightly on tortilla chips. Top with cheese and then black olives. Place 10 chips at a time on paper plate. Cook on 70 (roast) for 30 seconds or until cheese begins to melt.
2. Serve hot.

This is one of those "do it now" recipes. Be sure to spread the dip on the chips just before cooking or you might end up with soggy chips.

Toasted Seasoned Pecans

1 pound

1 pound pecan halves
1 tablespoon seasoned salt

¼ cup butter

1. Put pecans in a 1½-quart microproof casserole. Sprinkle with seasoned salt. Cut butter in 8 pieces and space evenly on top of pecans. Cook, uncovered, on HI (max. power) for 5 to 6 minutes.

This recipe works equally well with a half pound of pecans. Simply cut ingredients and cooking time in half. Say, you can use walnuts, cashews, or almonds, too! Or mix them. (We don't recommend roasting nuts in a shell.)

Liver and Sausage Paté

30 servings

1 pound chicken livers
½ pound mild Italian sausages
⅓ cup cubed onion
1 tablespoon bourbon
¼ cup heavy cream
½ teaspoon salt
¼ teaspoon nutmeg

Frosting:

1 package (8 ounces) cream cheese
1 package (3 ounces) cream cheese
2 tablespoons butter or margarine
1½ tablespoon cream

1. Butter a 7½- x 3¾- x 2½-inch loaf pan. After buttering, line bottom and sides with waxed paper or foil.
2. Rinse chicken livers under cold water, pat dry. Remove casing from sausages and break up meat.
3. Put sausages in 4-cup glass measure. Cover with waxed paper and cook on HI (max. power) for 4 minutes, or until sausages lose pinkness. Remove sausages and set aside.
4. Pierce each chicken liver with toothpick. Place in glass measure with sausage drippings. Cover and cook on HI (max. power) for 3 to 4 minutes, or until livers lose pinkness. Stir once during cooking.
5. Puree onion and bourbon in electric blender container. Add livers and sausages, heavy cream, and seasonings. Cover and blend on high speed. Stop blender and push ingredients toward blades, if necessary.
6. Pour into prepared loaf pan and refrigerate 12 hours or overnight. Unmold and frost about 2 hours before serving.

To frost loaf:

1. Soften cream cheese and butter together. (Remove foil wrap, place on microproof plate.) Cook on 50 (simmer) for 2 minutes.
2. Place softened cream cheese and butter, and the cream in electric blender container. Cover and blend on high until smooth and fluffy.
3. Loosen Paté and turn out on serving platter. Carefully remove waxed paper. Frost top and sides generously with cream cheese mixture. Refrigerate 1 hour, or until cheese is firm. Serve with assorted crackers.

SOUPS

Microwave preparation of homemade or prepared soups, stews, and chowders is so easy you'll find them on your menu more often. Long hours of simmering required in the conventional method are reduced to minutes. You will also want to prepare, and especially to heat, soups in individual serving dishes. Boilovers are more likely with heavy liquids, just as they are atop a conventional range; so, always select a large capacity microproof cooking utensil.

ADAPTING YOUR OWN RECIPES

Soup recipes convert very well and easily to the microwave method. It's really quite easy to find a recipe here with the approximate density and volume of the family favorite you want to try. You may have to alter an ingredient or two for success. Split pea soup, navy bean soup and others which use dried beans do not microwave well. However, canned, precooked navy beans are available and substitute well for dried. Some useful reminders:

- Soups are cooked covered. Microproof casserole lids, waxed paper, or plastic wrap may be used.
- Occasional stirring is desirable for even distribution of the ingredients and even cooking.
- HI (max. power) is the usual setting for soups with raw vegetables, fish, or seafood. Soups with uncooked meat and chicken soups start cooking at HI (max. power) and finish cooking at 50 (simmer). If ingredients are cooked meats and/or vegetables, 80 (reheat) is most often used. Soups with a milk or cream base use 70 (roast.)

USING THE COOKING GUIDES

Quick Soups

1. Put water in microproof mug or casserole.
2. Cover with waxed paper or casserole top.
3. Cook according to chart instructions.
4. Let stand 5 minutes before serving.
5. Check noodles or rice, if any. If not cooked, return to oven. Cook at 80 (reheat) for ½ minute.
6. Temperature probe may be used. Set at 200° and cook on HI (max. power).

Canned Soups

1. Pour soup into 1½-or-2-quart microproof casserole.
2. Add milk or water as directed. Stir.
3. Cover with casserole lid, waxed paper, or plastic wrap.
4. Temperature probe may be used. Set at 160° and cook on 80 (reheat).
5. Let stand, covered, 3 minutes before serving.

COOKING GUIDE — QUICK SOUPS

Soup	Number of Envelopes	Microproof Container	Cups of Water Each	Setting	Minutes
Cup of Soup 1½ ounces (4 envelopes)	1	1 (8-ounce) mug	⅔	HI (max. power)	2 to 2½
	2	2 (8-ounce) mugs	⅔	HI (max. power)	3 to 3½
	4	4 (8-ounce) mugs	⅔	HI (max. power)	6 to 7
Soup Mix without rice or noodles, 2¾–ounce packages (2 envelopes)	1	2-quart casserole	4	HI (max. power)	8 to 10

Soup	Microproof Casserole	Setting	Minutes
Broth	1½-quart	80 (reheat)	3½ to 4
Cream style: Tomato			
10¾ ounces	1½-quart	80 (reheat)	5 to 6
26 ounces	2-quart	80 (reheat)	8 to 10
Bean, Pea or Mushroom			
10¾ ounces	1½-quart	70 (roast)	7 to 8
Undiluted chunk style vegetable:			
10¾ ounces	1-quart	80 (reheat)	2½ to 4
19 ounces	1½-quart	80 (reheat)	5 to 7

Chili Chowder
6 servings

¾ pound lean ground beef
1 medium onion, chopped
1 clove garlic, chopped
2 tablespoons chopped green pepper
1 can (16 ounces) peeled plum tomatoes

2 cups tomato juice
1 teaspoon salt
⅛ teaspoon sugar
2 teaspoons chili powder, or to taste

1. Place beef, onion, garlic, and green pepper in a 2-quart microproof casserole. Cover and cook on HI (max. power) for 5 minutes.
2. Remove casserole and stir contents to break up beef, drain if necessary. Add tomatoes, including liquid from can, stirring to break up tomatoes.
3. Add remaining ingredients and mix well. Cover and cook on HI (max. power) for 7 to 9 minutes, or until hot.

Alternate method: The temperature probe may be used in Step 3. Cook on HI (max. power) set at 150°.

Canadian Green Pea Soup

4 to 6 servings

1 can (2 ounces) mushroom stems and pieces
1 tablespoon butter or margarine
2 cans (11½ ounces each) condensed green pea soup, undiluted

1 cup grated raw carrots
½ teaspoon salt

1. Drain mushroom liquid into a large measuring cup. Add enough water to make 2 cups of liquid. Melt butter in a 2-quart microproof casserole on 60 (bake) for 30 seconds.
2. Add mushrooms, soup, and mushroom-water mixture. Stir with fork until well blended. Stir in grated carrots and salt. Cover and cook on 80 (reheat) for 10 minutes, or just until carrots are tender.
3. Serve hot with croutons or crackers.

Alternate method: The temperature probe may be used in Step 2. Cook on HI (max. power) set at 150°.

Cream of Mushroom Soup

6 servings

2 cups chopped fresh mushrooms
½ teaspoon onion powder
⅛ teaspoon garlic powder
⅛ teaspoon white pepper

¼ teaspoon salt
2½ cups chicken broth
1 cup heavy cream

1. Combine mushrooms, seasonings, and broth in a 2-quart microproof casserole. Cook on HI (max. power) for 5 minutes, stirring once.
2. Stir in cream. Cook on 60 (bake) for 2 minutes, or until hot.

Alternate method: The temperature probe may be used for Step 2. Cook on 60 (bake) set at 150°.

Oyster Stew

4 to 6 servings

4 tablespoons butter or margarine
1 pint fresh oysters, drained; reserve liquid
3 cups milk

½ teaspoon salt
¼ teaspoon white pepper
Chopped chives

1. In 2-quart microproof casserole melt butter on HI (max. power) for 45 seconds.
2. Add drained oysters. Cover and cook on HI (max. power) for 4 to 5 minutes, or until edges curl.
3. Add milk, salt, pepper, and reserved liquid and cook on 50 (simmer) for 8 to 9 minutes, or until hot but not boiling.
4. Sprinkle with chives and serve.

Potato-Parsley Soup

4 to 6 servings

3 cups peeled, diced potatoes
¼ cup chopped onion
¼ teaspoon salt
1 can (13¾ ounces) chicken broth

1 cup chopped parsley, lightly packed
2 tablespoons cornstarch
1½ to 2 cups milk

1. Combine potatoes, onion, salt, and broth in a 2-quart microproof casserole. Add parsley. Cover, and cook on HI (max. power) 14 minutes, or until potatoes are tender.
2. Combine cornstarch with a small amount of cold milk. Stir into potato mixture. Add remaining milk. Cook, uncovered, on 70 (roast) for 3 to 4 minutes, or until soup is hot. Stir once during cooking time.

Alternate method: The temperature probe may be used in Step 2. Cook on 70 (roast) set at 150°.

Navy Bean and Bacon Soup

6 servings

8 slices bacon
2 tablespoons bacon drippings
1 large onion, chopped
1 clove garlic, minced

2 cans (15 ounces each) navy beans
½ teaspoon salt
1 can (8 ounces) tomato sauce

1. Cook bacon according to directions on page 56 until crisp. Crumble and set aside.
2. Place bacon drippings in a 2-quart microproof casserole. Add onion and garlic, stir. Cover and cook on HI (max. power) 2 minutes, or until onion is transparent.
3. Add ½ cup water and remaining ingredients including bean liquid. Mix well. Cover and cook on HI (max. power) for 5 to 6 minutes.
4. Puree soup in electric blender container, one-half of mixture at a time. Pour soup into a microproof soup tureen or large serving bowl. If thinner soup is desired, stir in additional water. Cover with waxed paper, cook on 70 (roast) for 4 minutes, or until hot. Stir once during cooking. Garnish with crumbled bacon before serving.

New England Clam Chowder

4 to 6 servings

2 slices bacon, diced
1 medium onion, chopped
2 medium potatoes, peeled and cubed
¼ cup butter
¼ cup all-purpose flour

2 cans (7½ ounces each) minced clams, drained; reserve liquid
3 cups milk
½ teaspoon salt
⅛ teaspoon white pepper

1. In 3-quart microproof casserole, cook bacon on HI (max. power) for 3 minutes.
2. Stir in onion and potatoes. Cover and cook on 90 (saute) for 8 to 10 minutes, or until potatoes are tender.

3. Melt butter in 2-cup glass measure on HI (max. power) for 1 minute. Stir in flour and add to potato mixture; mix well.
4. Add enough water to reserved clam juice to make 2 cups liquid. Stir this liquid, clams, and remaining ingredients into casserole. Cover and cook on HI (max. power) for 4 to 5 minutes, or until hot.

Alternate method: The temperature probe may be used for Step 4. Cook on 60 (bake) set at 150°.

Hearty Cheese Soup

4 servings

¼ cup butter or margarine	Pinch pepper
¼ cup chopped onion	2½ cups milk
1 medium carrot grated (about ¾ cup)	2 cups shredded sharp Cheddar cheese
¼ cup all-purpose flour	
¼ teaspoon salt	½ cup beer

1. Place butter, onion, and carrots in 2-quart microproof casserole. Cook on 90 (saute) 3 minutes, or until onions are transparent. Blend in flour and seasonings.
2. Heat milk in 4-cup glass measure on 70 (roast) for 4 minutes. Gradually add milk to vegetable-flour mixture, stirring constantly. Cook on 70 (roast) for 5 minutes, stirring after each minute until thickened.
3. Add cheese; stir until melted. Add beer. Cook on 70 (roast) for 2 minutes, or until hot, not boiling.

Another of those microwave niceties! In Step 2, leave a wooden spoon in the casserole – in the oven – for stirring. The spoon won't get hot and it's always handy.

Mock Lobster Bisque

6 servings

1 package (16 ounces) frozen codfish fillets	1 can (10¾ ounces) pea soup
	½ cup sherry
1 can (10¾ ounces) tomato soup	1¼ cups milk

1. Defrost codfish in package for 8 minutes on 30 (defrost). Separate fillets under cold water.
2. On 9-inch microproof pie plate, place fish fillets with thickest area to outside edge of dish. Cover with well-dampened paper towel. Cook on HI (max. power) for 4 minutes.
3. In a 3-quart microproof casserole, mix soups, sherry, and milk. Mix until pea soup is dissolved. Flake fish with fork, watch for and discard any bones. Add fish and drainings, if any, to soup mixture. Cover and cook on 50 (simmer) for 10 minutes, or until hot but not boiling. Stir once during cooking.

Cioppino Supreme

8 servings

1 large onion, chopped
1 medium green pepper, seeded and chopped
½ cup thinly sliced celery
3 cloves garlic, minced
3 tablespoons olive oil
1 can (1 pound 12 ounces) Italian tomatoes
1 can (8 ounces) tomato sauce
1 teaspoon basil
1 bay leaf

1 teaspoon salt
¼ teaspoon pepper
1 pound firm white fish
1 dozen mussels or littleneck clams in the shell
1 to 1½ cups dry white wine
½ pound whole shrimp, cleaned and deveined
½ pound scallops
1 lobster tail (6 ounces), cut into chunks

1. Combine onion, pepper, celery, garlic, and olive oil in a 4-quart microproof casserole. Cook on 90 (saute) for about 5 minutes, or until onion is transparent.
2. Break tomatoes into small pieces with spoon. Add tomatoes, tomato sauce, basil, bay leaf, salt, and pepper to casserole. Cover and cook on HI (max. power) for 15 minutes to blend flavors.
3. While sauce is cooking, cut white fish into serving pieces. Scrub mussels or clams and soak in cold water.
4. Stir wine into tomato mixture. Add white fish, shrimp, scallops, and lobster. Cover and cook on HI (max. power) for 10 minutes.
5. Place mussels or clams in a layer on top of fish in casserole. Cover and cook on HI (max. power) for 10 minutes. Discard any unopened mussels or clams.
6. Serve hot with French bread.

Corn Chowder

6 to 8 servings

4 slices bacon
1 small onion, chopped fine
¼ cup chopped green pepper
2 cans (16 ounces each) cream style corn

1 can (10¾ ounces) cream of potato soup, undiluted
2 cups milk
1 teaspoon salt
¼ teaspoon pepper

1. Cook bacon according to directions on page 56. Crumble bacon and set aside.
2. Put 2 tablespoons of bacon drippings in 4-quart microproof casserole, stir in onion and green pepper. Cook on 90 (saute) for 3 minutes, or until onion is transparent.
3. Stir in all remaining ingredients. Cover and cook on 50 (simmer) for 16 to 18 minutes, or until hot. Stir twice during cooking.
4. Sprinkle crumbled bacon on top of chowder and serve.

Corn Chowder can make Sunday night supper special with side dishes of crumbled bacon, minced parsley, chopped peanuts, and chopped hard-cooked eggs. All can help themselves to the toppings they prefer.

Garden Vegetable Soup

4 to 6 servings

2 tablespoons butter or margarine
2 bunches green onion, thinly sliced
1 small onion, sliced
1 cup sliced celery
1 large carrot, sliced (about 1 cup)
1 medium turnip, peeled and cubed

1 large potato, peeled and cubed
2 cans (14 ounces each) regular strength chicken broth, divided
¼ teaspoon marjoram
½ teaspoon salt
⅛ teaspoon white pepper

1. Melt butter in 4-quart microproof casserole on HI (max. power) for 1 minute.
2. Stir in green onion, onion, celery, and carrot. Cover and cook on HI (max. power) for 10 minutes, or until celery is soft.
3. Stir in turnip and potato and ½ cup broth. Cover and cook on HI (max. power) for 13 minutes, or until potato is tender; stir twice during cooking time.
4. Stir in remaining broth and marjoram. In electric blender container, puree one-half of mixture at a time, transfer to microproof soup tureen or large serving bowl. Add salt and pepper.
5. Cover tureen or serving bowl with waxed paper and heat soup on HI (max. power) 5 to 8 minutes, or until hot.

Minestrone Soup

6 to 8 servings

1 pound beef chuck
5 cups hot water
1 medium onion, chopped
¼ teaspoon pepper
½ teaspoon basil
1 clove garlic, minced
½ cup thinly sliced carrots
1 can (16 ounces) tomatoes
½ cup uncooked vermicelli, broken into 1 inch pieces

1½ cups sliced zucchini
1 can (16 ounces) kidney beans, drained
1 cup shredded cabbage
2 tablespoons chopped parsley
1 teaspoon salt
Grated Parmesan or Romano cheese

1. Trim meat by removing fat and gristle, cut into ½- to ¾-inch pieces. Put meat in 4-quart microproof casserole, pour water over meat; add onion, pepper, basil, and garlic. Cover and cook on HI (max. power) for 25 minutes, or until meat is tender.
2. Add carrots and tomatoes. Cover and cook on HI (max. power) for 8 minutes.
3. Stir in vermicelli, zucchini, beans, cabbage, parsley, and salt. Cover and cook on HI (max. power) for 10 minutes; stir once.
4. Allow to stand 5 minutes before serving. Sprinkle generously with cheese.

French Onion Soup

6 to 8 servings

3 large onions, thinly sliced and quartered
¼ cup butter or margarine
2 teaspoons all-purpose flour
6 cups regular strength beef broth
¼ cup dry white wine
½ teaspoon salt
⅛ teaspoon white pepper
   Garlic powder
6 to 8 slices French bread, toasted and buttered
1 cup shredded Swiss cheese

1. Cook onion and butter in covered 3-quart microproof casserole on HI (max. power) for 10 to 12 minutes, or until onions are transparent.
2. Stir in flour and cook, uncovered, on HI (max. power) for 1 minute.
3. Stir in broth, wine, salt, and pepper. Cover and cook on HI (max. power) for 8 minutes.
4. To serve, lightly sprinkle garlic powder on hot buttered toast. Nearly fill microproof soup bowls with hot soup; float toast on top. Cover toast generously with Swiss cheese. Place 2 bowls (or 3, in a circle) in microwave oven. Cook, uncovered on 70 (roast) for 2 minutes, or until cheese is melted.

You may prefer to prepare this soup early in the day. If so, refrigerate after Step 3. Later, cover and cook on HI (max. power) for 18 to 20 minutes, stirring twice during heating. Then continue with Step 4.

MEATS

Microwave meat cookery offers tremendous advantages over conventional methods. It stretches your meat dollar by reducing shrinkage. You can defrost, cook, and reheat. Meats for the barbecue, too, are enhanced by pre-cooking in the microwave. Microwave roasting methods are like dry roasting in your conventional oven. This means that the better, tender cuts of meat are recommended for best results. Less tender cuts of meat are best when marinated or tenderized and are cooked at very low power settings. They can also be braised. Some people insist meat does not brown in microwave ovens. Wrong! Any meat which cooks more than 10 minutes will brown in your microwave oven. True, individual steaks, ground meat patties, chops, and thin cuts of meat brown best with a microwave browning dish or grill dish.

ADAPTING YOUR OWN RECIPES

You should not have any trouble locating your favorite cut of meat in the charts. For most, the temperature probe eliminates any guesswork or troublesome arithmetic. True budget cuts, which depend upon especially long cooking times to develop tenderness and flavor, do not microwave well. For casseroles, stuffed meats, meats in sauces, loaves, and such recipes, you're sure to find a similar recipe here. Adapt your conventional recipes by matching ingredients and methods as closely as possible the first time; then experiment the next time. Some good things to know:

- Evenly shaped, boned, rolled, and tied small roasts (3 to 6 pounds) cook best.
- Recipe times here presume meat is thawed but at refrigerator temperature. If your recipe requires lengthy preparation which may see meat reach room temperature, consider reducing cooking times. (The temperature probe eliminates concern.)
- Cover casserole dishes tightly to enhance flavor and tenderness.
- Check dishes which use relatively long cooking times regularly to be sure liquid has not evaporated; add liquid, if necessary.

USING THE DEFROSTING GUIDE

1. You may defrost meats within original paper or plastic wrappings. Remove all metal rings, twist ties, or wire. Remove all foil wrapping.
2. Place meat in microproof dish.
3. Defrost only as long as necessary. Separate items like chops, bacon slices, and wieners into pieces as soon as possible. Remove if almost thawed. Continue to defrost remaining pieces. If separated pieces are not thawed, distribute them evenly in oven and continue.
4. Slightly increase the time for weights larger than on the chart. Do not double.
5. If you are defrosting other than for immediate cooking, follow the recommended method for one-half to three-fourths of recommended time. Place in refrigerator until needed.

USING THE COOKING GUIDE

1. Meats should be thawed before cooking.
2. Place meat, fat side down, on microwave roasting rack set in glass baking dish. An inverted microproof saucer may be used if you do not have a microwave roasting rack.
3. Turn meat halfway through cooking time; set second setting and continue cooking.

Rolled Rib Roast

4. Meat may be covered lightly with waxed paper to stop splatters.
5. Use the temperature probe for accurate roasting.
6. Irregular meat cuts have areas which cook faster than others. When smaller end is done, cover with small piece of aluminum foil while thicker, heavier sections continue to cook. Be sure aluminum foil is at least 1 inch from oven walls.

7. Ground meat for casseroles is best crumbled into a microproof dish and cooked covered with a paper towel; then, drain and prepare casserole.
8. During standing time, the internal temperature of roasts will rise approximately 15°. Hence, standing time is considered part of the time required to complete cooking.

COOKING GUIDE—MEATS

Meat	First Setting and Time	Second Setting and Time	Meat Probe Setting	Minutes Standing Time
	Turn meat between first and second settings			
Beef				
Ground beef	HI (max. power) 2½ minutes per lb.	HI (max. power) 2½ minutes per lb.		
Ground beef* 4 ¼-pound patties	HI (max. power) 2½ to 3 minutes Then turn over.	HI (max. power) 3 to 5½ minutes		
Meat loaf 2 pounds	70 (roast) 25 to 30 minutes	none	140°	
Rib roast, rolled	HI (max. power) Rare: 4 to 5 mins. per lb. Med.: 5 to 6 mins. per lb. Well: 6 to 7 mins. per lb.	70 (roast) 3 to 4 mins. per lb. 5 to 6 mins. per lb. 6 to 7 mins. per lb.	125° 135° 155°	4 to 5 5 to 8 8 to 12
Rib roast, bone in	HI (max. power) Rare: 3 to 4 mins. per lb. Med.: 4 to 5 mins. per lb. Well: 5 to 6 mins. per lb.	70 (roast) 3 to 4 mins. per lb. 3 to 5 mins. per lb. 5 to 6 mins. per lb.	125° 135° 155°	4 to 5 5 to 8 8 to 12
Rump roast or chuck pot roast (cook, covered, in a liquid)	HI (max. power) 5 minutes per pound	50 (simmer) 10 minutes per pound		12 to 15
Round steak (in liquid)	HI (max. power) 5 minutes per pound	50 (simmer) 15 minutes per pound		8 to 10
Sirloin steak*	HI (max. power) 4½ minutes per pound	none		
Minute steak* 4 6-ounce steaks	HI (max. power) 2 to 4 minutes	none		
Tenderloin* 4 8-ounce steaks	HI (max. power) Rare: 5 to 7 minutes Med.: 8 to 11 minutes Well: 10 to 12 minutes	none	125° 135° 155°	2 to 4 4 to 8 10 to 12

COOKING GUIDE—MEATS

Meat	First Setting and Time	Second Setting and Time	Meat Probe Setting	Minutes Standing Time
	Turn meat between first and second settings			
Lamb				
Cubed (in liquid)	Follow lamb recipes	none.		
Roast	70 (roast) 5 to 6 minutes per pound	70 (roast) 5 to 6 minutes per pound	150°	
Chops*	HI (max. power) 5 to 6 minutes per pound			
Leg (cover bone end with aluminum foil for one-half cooking time)	70 (roast) Med.: 4 to 5 mins. per lb. Well: 5 to 6 mins. per lb.	70 (roast) Med.: 4 to 5 mins. per lb. Well: 5 to 6 mins. per lb.	145° 165°	0 to 5 5 to 10
Pork				
Chops* 4 medium chops	HI (max. power) 8 to 9 minutes	none		0 to 5
Spareribs	70 (roast) 6 to 7 minutes per pound	70 (roast) 6 to 7 minutes per pound		
Roast	HI (max. power) 5 to 6 minutes per pound	HI (max. power) 5 to 6 minutes per pound	155°	10
Ham Boneless, ready-to-eat	70 (roast) 5 to 7 minutes per pound	70 (roast) 5 to 7 minutes per pound	120°	5 to 10
Shank of Leg	70 (roast) 4 to 5 minutes per pound	70 (roast) 4 to 5 minutes per pound	120°	
Canned 3 pound	70 (roast) 5 to 6 minutes per pound	70 (roast) 5 to 6 minutes per pound	120°	
5 pound	70 (roast) 4 to 5 minutes per pound	70 (roast) 4 to 5 minutes per pound	120°	
Sausage patties* 4 1-pound patties	HI (max. power) 4 to 5 minutes	HI (max. power) 4 to 5 minutes		
Veal				
Roast	70 (roast) 4 to 6 minutes per pound	70 (roast) 4 to 6 minutes per pound	155°	0 to 10
Chops	Check recipe section			

*Use a browning dish if desired.
 Cooking time may need to be reduced.

DEFROSTING GUIDE—MEATS

Meat	Minutes per Pound	Setting	Minutes Standing Time	Special Notes
Beef				
Ground beef: 1 pound round block	5 to 6	30 (defrost)	5	Freeze in doughnut shape. Turn over once. Remove thawed portions with fork. Return remainder.
Ground beef patty: ¼ pound	1 per patty	30 (defrost)	2	Defrost on plate. Depress center when freezing.
Pot roast, chuck: 4 pounds and under over 4 pounds	3 to 5 3 to 5	30 (defrost) 70 (roast)	10 10	Turn over once. Turn over once.
Rib roast, rolled: 3 to 4 pounds 6 to 8 pounds	6 to 8 6 to 8	30 (defrost) 70 (roast)	30 to 45 90	Turn over once. Turn over twice.
Rib roast, bone in	5 to 6	70 (roast)	45 to 90	Turn over twice.
Rump roast: 3 to 4 pounds 6 to 7 pounds	3 to 5 3 to 5	30 (defrost) 70 (roast)	30 45	Turn over once. Turn over twice.
Round steak	4 to 5	30 (defrost)	5 to 10	Turn over once.
Flank steak	4 to 5	30 (defrost)	5 to 10	Turn over once.
Sirloin steak: ½ inch thick	4 to 5	30 (defrost)	5 to 10	Turn over once.
Lunch meat: 8 ounce package	1 to 2	30 (defrost)		Until pieces separate.
Steaks: 2 or 3 per package, 2 to 3 pounds	4 to 5	30 (defrost)	8 to 10	Turn over once.
Stew meat: 2 pounds	3 to 5	30 (defrost)	8 to 10	Turn over once. Separate with fork.
Lamb				
Cubed	7 to 8	30 (defrost)	5	Break up cubes halfway through defrosting time with fork.
Roast: 4 pounds and under over 4 pounds	3 to 5 3 to 5	30 (defrost) 70 (roast)	30 to 45 30 to 45	Turn over once. Turn over twice.
Chops: 4 1 inch thick	5 to 8	30 (defrost)	15	Turn over twice.
Leg: 5 to 8 pounds	4 to 5	30 (defrost)	15 to 20	Turn over twice.

DEFROSTING GUIDE—MEATS

Meat	Minutes per Pound	Setting	Minutes Standing Time	Special Notes
Pork				
Chops	4 to 6	30 (defrost)	5 to 10	Separate chops halfway through defrosting time. Add 1 more minute if needed.
Spareribs	5 to 7	30 (defrost)	10	
Roast:				
4 pounds and under	4 to 5	30 (defrost)	30 to 45	Turn over once.
over 4 pounds	4 to 5	70 (roast)	30 to 45	Turn over twice.
Bacon:				
1 pound package	2 to 3	30 (defrost)	3 to 5	Until strips separate.
Sausage, bulk:				
1 pound package	2 to 3	30 (defrost)	3 to 5	Turn over once. Remove thawed portions with fork. Return remainder.
Sausage links:				
1 pound package	3 to 5	30 (defrost)	4 to 6	Turn over once. Until pieces can be separated.
Veal				
Roast:				
3 to 4 pounds	5 to 7	30 (defrost)	30	Turn over once.
6 to 7 pounds	5 to 7	70 (roast)	90	Turn over twice.
Chops	4 to 6	30 (defrost)	20	Turn over once. Separate chops and continue defrosting.

Yankee Pot Roast

about 6 servings

1 3-pound beef chuck pot roast
½ cup dry red wine
½ cup beef broth
2 large onions, thinly sliced

3 medium potatoes, cut in quarters
4 carrots, peeled and sliced
1 teaspoon salt
¼ teaspoon pepper

1. Place pot roast in a 3-quart microproof casserole. Add wine and beef broth; cover with sliced onions. Cover and cook on HI (max. power) for 4 minutes.
2. Cook on 50 (simmer) for 1½ hours. If liquid is low, add additional beef broth.
3. Add potatoes, carrots, salt, and pepper. Cover and cook on 50 (simmer) for 45 minutes, or until vegetables and meat are tender.
4. Let stand, covered, 5 to 10 minutes before serving.

New England Boiled Dinner

8 to 10 servings

1 3-pound corned beef brisket
1 bay leaf
½ teaspoon whole black peppercorns
2 cloves garlic
4 whole cloves

2 medium onions, quartered
3 carrots, peeled and sliced
3 potatoes, peeled and quartered
1 very small cabbage, cut into 8 wedges

1. Place corned beef in a 3- to 4-quart microproof casserole or baking dish. Add bay leaf, peppercorns, garlic, cloves, 2 cups water, and onions. Cover and cook on HI (max. power) for 15 minutes.
2. Turn meat over and cook on 50 (simmer) for 30 minutes. Turn meat over and cook on 50 (simmer) for 30 minutes, or until meat is almost tender.
3. Add carrots, potatoes, and cabbage wedges. Cover and cook on 50 (simmer) for 30 minutes, or until meat and vegetables are tender.
4. Let stand 5 minutes before slicing meat.

Beef Stroganoff

3 to 4 servings

1 pound beef sirloin steak, cut in very thin strips
1 large onion, chopped
1 beef bouillon cube
1 tablespoon all-purpose flour

1 teaspoon catsup
½ teaspoon salt
½ cup dairy sour cream
Hot cooked rice or noodles

1. Combine beef strips, onion, bouillon cube, flour, catsup, salt, and ½ cup water in a 1-quart microproof casserole or baking dish. Stir well. Cover and cook on HI (max. power) for 4 minutes. Stir well. Cover and cook on 70 (roast) for 6 minutes, or until meat is tender.
2. Stir in sour cream. Cook on 10 (warm) for 3 minutes.
3. Let stand 3 minutes. Serve with hot cooked rice or noodles.

You'll find this popular favorite easier to prepare if you freeze the steak for about 30 minutes first. Then slice at once. The steak strips will be thinner and more uniform. It's also nice to brown the steak strips first using a microwave browning dish in your microwave oven.

Oriental Beef

4 to 6 servings

1½ to 2 pounds thinly cut boneless sirloin steak, cut into thin strips
½ cup soy sauce
½ cup dry sherry
1 tablespoon sugar
1 whole clove garlic, cut in half
2 thin slices gingerroot
1 bunch green onions
1 can (5 ounces) sliced water chestnuts
½ bunch fresh broccoli or one package (10 ounces) frozen broccoli spears, thawed
½ pound fresh bean sprouts or 2 cups canned bean sprouts

1. Combine steak, soy sauce, sherry, ¼ cup water, sugar, garlic, and ginger in a 12- x 7-inch microproof baking dish. Cover with plastic wrap and let stand at room temperature 4 hours. Occasionally uncover and turn meat over.
2. Clean green onions and cut into 2-inch pieces. Drain water from chestnuts. Cut broccoli stems into thin slices; leave flowerets whole. Rinse bean sprouts.
3. Remove garlic and ginger from meat. Push meat to center of dish. Place some of each vegetable in each corner of the baking dish and then around meat. Cover dish with plastic wrap.
4. Cook on HI (max. power) for 10 to 12 minutes. Remove from oven and let stand 2 minutes.
5. Serve with hot cooked rice.

Gingerroot should be easily available in the produce section of your store. However, 1 teaspoon ground ginger may be substituted. It then stays in the dish, of course, and can't be removed in Step 3.

Beef and Peppers

4 servings

2 tablespoons cooking oil
1 pound top round or sirloin steak, cut into thin strips
1 medium onion, finely chopped
1 clove garlic, minced
1 teaspoon salt
⅛ teaspoon pepper
1 can (16 ounces) tomatoes, broken up
2 large green peppers, seeded and cut in strips
2 tablespoons soy sauce

1. Put oil in 3-quart microproof casserole or baking dish. Add beef strips and stir to coat with oil. Add onion, garlic, salt, pepper, and tomatoes.
2. Cover and cook on HI (max. power) for 4 minutes, stirring once during cooking time.
3. Add green peppers and soy sauce, stir. Cover and cook on HI (max. power) for 4 to 5 minutes, or just until green pepper is tender.
4. Serve with hot cooked rice or chow mein noodles.

Beef Stew

4 to 6 servings

2 pounds stew beef, cut in 1-inch cubes
½ teaspoon salt
1 package (1½ ounces) brown gravy mix with mushrooms

3 stalks celery, cut in 1-inch slices
3 medium carrots, peeled and sliced
3 medium potatoes, peeled and cut in eighths

1. Put beef cubes in a 3-quart microproof casserole or baking dish. Sprinkle with salt. Combine gravy mix with 1 cup water. Stir. Pour over meat. Cover and cook on HI (max. power) for 5 minutes. Stir. Cover and cook on 60 (bake) for 20 minutes.
2. Add celery, carrots, and potatoes and stir lightly so that vegetables are covered with gravy. Add more water for a thinner gravy and salt for the vegetables. Cover and cook on 50 (simmer) for 25 to 30 minutes, or until vegetables and meat are tender.
3. Remove and let stand 5 minutes.

Beef Goulash

4 to 6 servings

2 pounds stew beef, cut in 1-inch cubes
3 to 4 large tomatoes
1 onion, coarsely chopped

1 teaspoon salt
½ teaspoon freshly ground pepper
1 cup dairy sour cream

1. Place beef in a 3-quart microproof casserole. Peel tomatoes; remove cores. Cut tomatoes in chunks. Place in casserole with beef, onion, salt, and pepper. Stir.
2. Cover and cook on 70 (roast) for 40 to 45 minutes, or until beef is tender. Stir twice during cooking time.
3. Stir sour cream into mixture and let stand, covered, 5 minutes.

This is excellent served with cooked egg noodles. Biscuits or rice are fine, too.

Short Ribs of Beef

4 servings

2 pounds meaty short ribs of beef
1 clove garlic, minced
½ teaspoon salt

½ cup dry red wine
1 tablespoon browning sauce

1. Arrange short ribs in a 3-quart microproof casserole. Sprinkle with garlic and salt. Combine wine and browning sauce. Pour over short ribs.
2. Cover with plastic wrap and cook on 70 (roast) for about 30 minutes, or until meat is tender.
3. Remove and let stand 5 minutes.

Shish Kabob

6 to 8 servings

½ cup wine vinegar
½ cup cooking oil
1 teaspoon onion salt
1 clove garlic, split in half
¼ cup soy sauce
2 teaspoons Italian seasoning

2 pounds boneless sirloin or lamb
½ pound small fresh mushrooms
1 dozen tomato wedges or cherry
tomatoes
1 green pepper, seeded and cut in
1-inch squares

1. Make a marinade by combining vinegar, oil, onion salt, garlic, soy sauce, Italian seasoning, and ½ cup water in a large mixing bowl. Cut steak in 1-inch cubes. Add to marinade and let stand at room temperature 5 to 6 hours.
2. Place meat cubes and vegetables alternately on long wooden skewers. Place 2 or 3 skewers on a microproof dinner plate.
3. Cook, uncovered, on 30 (defrost) for 6 minutes for medium rare. Cook slightly longer for well done meat.

You may use wooden or metal skewers for your kabobs. If using metal skewers, be especially careful not to allow them to touch the wall of the oven.

Tomato Swiss Steak

4 servings

¼ cup all-purpose flour
1 teaspoon salt
¼ teaspoon pepper
1½ to 2 pounds round steak

2 large onions, sliced
1 green pepper, cut in strips
1 can (10¾ ounces) beef broth
1 can (10½ ounces) tomato puree

1. Combine flour, salt, and pepper. Place steak on a cutting board and pound half of the flour mixture into each side of the steak with meat mallet or edge of saucer. Cut meat in 4 pieces and place in an 8-inch square or 11- x 7-inch microproof baking dish. Sprinkle remaining flour mixture over meat. Spread onions, peppers, and tomato puree over meat. Pour broth to cover meat. Cover with waxed paper and cook on HI (max. power) for 5 minutes.
2. Cook on 60 (bake) for 40 minutes.
3. Rearrange meat and cook on 60 (bake) for 10 minutes, or until meat is tender.

Chili con Carne

4 servings

1 pound lean ground beef
¼ cup minced onion
½ cup chopped green pepper
1 clove garlic, minced
1 to 2 tablespoons chili powder

1 teaspoon salt
1 can (16 ounces) tomatoes,
undrained
1 can (16 ounces) kidney beans,
undrained

1. Crumble ground beef into a 2-quart microproof casserole or baking dish. Add onion, green pepper, and garlic. Cook, uncovered, on HI (max. power) for 4 minutes. Drain meat and break up with a fork.
2. Add remaining ingredients. Cover and cook on 70 (roast) for 15 to 18 minutes, or until hot. Stir once during cooking time.
3. Let stand 5 minutes before serving.

Beef Rolls

6 servings

- 2 pounds beef top round steak, cut ½-inch thick
- 2 tablespoons butter or margarine
- ½ cup chopped celery with leaves
- ¼ cup chopped onion
- 1 cup soft bread crumbs
- ¼ teaspoon crushed rosemary
- ¼ teaspoon thyme
- ¼ teaspoon pepper
- 1 can (10¾ ounces) condensed cream of mushroom soup, undiluted

1. Pound steak with meat mallet or edge of saucer. Cut into 6 pieces. Combine butter, celery, and onion in a 1-quart glass measure. Cook on HI (max. power) for 4 minutes, or until onion is transparent.
2. Stir in bread crumbs, rosemary, thyme, and pepper. Divide stuffing among pieces of steak. Roll meat around stuffing and fasten with toothpicks. Arrange in a microproof baking dish. Spoon soup over top of meat rolls.
3. Cook on 70 (roast) for 30 minutes, or until meat is tender. Turn meat once during cooking time, spooning sauce over top of meat rolls.
4. Let stand 5 minutes before serving.

Cabbage Rolls

6 to 8 servings

- 1 head cabbage, about 1½ pounds
- 1 pound lean ground beef
- ½ pound ground pork
- ¾ cup cooked rice
- 1 egg, lightly beaten
- 1 teaspoon thyme
- 1 tablespoon chopped parsley
- 1 clove garlic, minced
- 2 teaspoons salt
- ¼ teaspoon pepper
- ¼ cup butter or margarine
- 1 can (16 ounces) tomato sauce

1. Remove core from cabbage. Remove any blemished leaves. Put cabbage in a 3-quart microproof casserole. Add ¼ cup water. Cover with plastic wrap and cook on HI (max. power) for 6 minutes.
2. Cool cabbage slightly. Separate leaves. Remove tough centers from 6 to 8 of the large outside leaves.
3. Combine ground beef, pork, rice, egg, thyme, parsley, garlic, salt, and pepper; mix. Divide mixture among the 6 to 8 large cabbage leaves. Wrap leaves tightly around mixture.
4. Line bottom of a 3-quart microproof casserole with some of the leftover cabbage leaves. Place cabbage rolls on top of loose leaves. Cover with remaining cabbage. Top with butter. Pour tomato sauce over top. Cover and cook on 80 (reheat) for about 30 minutes, or until meat is cooked and rolls are fork-tender.
5. Remove and let stand, covered, 5 minutes. Discard the top loose cabbage leaves before serving.

Beef Tacos

7 to 8 servings

1 pound lean ground beef
½ cup chopped onion
1 package (1¼ ounces)
  taco-seasoning mix
½ cup tomato juice

7 to 8 cooked taco shells
2 cups shredded lettuce
2 medium tomatoes, chopped
  Grated Cheddar cheese
  Diced avocado

1. Crumble beef into a 2-quart microproof casserole, add onion and cook, uncovered, on HI (max. power) for 4 minutes. Stir with a fork to break up meat; drain fat.
2. Stir in dry taco-seasoning mix and tomato juice. Cover with paper towel and cook on 70 (roast) for 6 minutes, or until hot.
3. Heat taco shells on paper towel or paper plate on HI (max. power) for 30 seconds.
4. Fill shells with ground beef mixture, lettuce, tomatoes, cheese, and avocado.

Beef and Rice Casserole

6 to 8 servings

1 pound lean ground beef
1 can (16 ounces) stewed tomatoes
1 can (16 ounces) cut green beans, undrained
½ cup uncooked rice
1 tablespoon instant minced onion

1 tablespoon sugar
1 teaspoon salt
1 teaspoon Worcestershire sauce
½ teaspoon dry mustard
⅛ teaspoon garlic powder
⅛ teaspoon pepper

1. Crumble ground beef into 2-quart microproof casserole. Cover with waxed paper and cook on HI (max. power) for 5 to 6 minutes. Stir once during cooking time to break up pieces. Drain fat.
2. Stir in all remaining ingredients. Cover and cook on HI (max. power) for 9 to 10 minutes, or until mixture boils.
3. Stir mixture, cover, and cook on 20 (low) for 10 minutes.
4. Stir, cover, and cook on 70 (roast) for 5 minutes, or until rice is tender and liquid absorbed.
5. Let stand 5 minutes before serving.

Favorite Meat Loaf

6 servings

1 can (8 ounces) tomato sauce
¼ cup brown sugar
¼ cup vinegar
1 teaspoon prepared mustard
1 egg, lightly beaten

1 medium onion, minced
¼ cup cracker crumbs
2 pounds lean ground beef
1½ teaspoons salt
¼ teaspoon pepper

1. Combine tomato sauce, brown sugar, vinegar, and mustard in a small bowl. Set aside.
2. Combine egg, onion, cracker crumbs, ground beef, salt, and pepper in a mixing bowl. Add ½ cup of the tomato mixture and blend thoroughly. Shape into an oval loaf and place in an oblong microproof baking dish. Make a depression in top of loaf. Pour remaining tomato sauce over top of meat.
3. Cook, uncovered, on 70 (roast) for 25 to 30 minutes, or until center is cooked.
4. Cover meat and let stand about 10 minutes before serving.

Alternate method: If using temperature probe, insert in center of meat loaf. Cook on 70 (roast) set at 140°. Cover and let stand 5 to 10 minutes before serving.

Onion Meatballs

6 servings

1½ pounds lean ground beef
½ cup milk
1 package (1¼ ounces) onion soup mix, divided

3 tablespoons all-purpose flour
2 tablespoons chopped parsley
½ cup dairy sour cream

1. In a large bowl, combine beef with milk and 2 tablespoons of the onion soup mix. Mix thoroughly. Shape into 24 meatballs. Place in a 3-quart oblong microproof baking dish. Cover with waxed paper and cook on HI (max. power) for 3 minutes.
2. Turn meatballs over. Cover and cook on HI (max. power) for 2 minutes.
3. Remove meatballs. Stir flour into drippings in dish. Stir in 1½ cups water, parsley, and remaining soup mix.
4. Cook, uncovered, on 60 (bake) for about 5 minutes, or until mixture comes to a boil.
5. Add meatballs. Cover and cook on 60 (bake) for 6 minutes, stirring occasionally during cooking time.
6. Gradually blend in sour cream. Cover and let stand 5 minutes before serving.
7. Serve over rice or noodles.

Leg of Lamb

8 servings

1 4- to 4½-pound leg of lamb, bone in   1 large clove garlic, thinly sliced

1. Cut small slits in both sides of leg of lamb. Insert thin slices of garlic in slits.
2. Place leg of lamb, fat side down, on a microwave roasting rack in a 12- x 7-inch microproof baking dish.
3. Cook, uncovered, on HI (max. power) for 25 minutes.
4. Turn lamb over with fat side up. Insert temperature probe in thickest part of leg, making sure not to touch the bone. Cook, uncovered, on 70 (roast) set at 165°.
5. Cover with aluminum foil and let stand about 10 minutes before serving.

You'll find a microwave roasting rack to be an often-used and convenient accessory. However, if you don't have one, use an inverted microproof saucer as a substitute.

Lamb Stew

4 servings

1 pound boneless lamb, cut in 1-inch cubes
1 package (⅝ ounces) brown gravy mix
2 tablespoons all-purpose flour
1 teaspoon salt
⅛ teaspoon pepper

1 clove garlic, minced
½ teaspoon Worcestershire sauce
¼ cup red wine
3 medium carrots, peeled and cut in chunks
2 stalks celery, cut in pieces
2 potatoes, peeled and cut in cubes

1. In a 3-quart microproof casserole combine lamb and gravy mix. Cook, uncovered, on HI (max. power) for 5 minutes, stirring once during cooking time.
2. Add remaining ingredients and 1 cup water. Stir well. Cover and cook on 60 (bake) for 20 to 25 minutes, or until meat and vegetables are tender. Stir once during cooking time.
3. Let stand 3 to 4 minutes before serving.

Zesty Lamb Chops

4 servings

4 shoulder lamb chops
½ cup coarsely chopped onion
1 clove garlic, minced

½ cup catsup
2 tablespoons Worcestershire sauce
1 tablespoon prepared mustard

1. In a microproof baking dish arrange lamb chops in one layer. Sprinkle with onion and garlic. Cook, uncovered, on HI (max. power) for 5 minutes.
2. Combine remaining ingredients and spread over lamb chops. Cover with waxed paper and cook on 60 (bake) for 15 minutes, or until lamb chops are tender.

Following pages: Left, Stuffed Pork Chops (recipe, p. 52); right, Barbecued Spareribs (recipe, p. 53)

Loin of Pork

6 to 8 servings

1 loin of pork, about 4 pounds

1. Place roast, fat side down, on a microwave roasting rack in a 12- x 7-inch microproof baking dish. Cook, uncovered, on HI (max. power) for 10 minutes.
2. Turn loin of pork, fat side up. Cover lightly with a piece of waxed paper and cook on 60 (bake) for 10 to 12 minutes per pound.
3. Let stand 10 minutes before serving.

Alternate Method: The temperature probe may be used in Step 2. Insert temperature probe in thickest part of meat, making sure that it does not touch bone or fat pocket. Cover with waxed paper and cook on 70 (roast) set at 155°.

Stuffed Pork Chops *(Illustrated on page 50)*

4 servings

1 cup coarse dry bread crumbs
¾ cup chopped apples
3 tablespoons chopped raisins
½ teaspoon salt
2 tablespoons sugar
2 tablespoons minced onion
¼ teaspoon pepper
Pinch sage
2 tablespoons melted butter or margarine
8 thin rib or loin pork chops
½ package (⅜ ounces) brown gravy mix

1. Combine bread crumbs, apples, raisins, salt, sugar, onion, pepper, sage, and melted butter. Mix lightly. Moisten slightly with hot water if stuffing is dry.
2. Trim all fat from pork chops. Place 4 chops in bottom of an 8-inch square microproof baking dish. Divide stuffing into 4 portions and place 1 portion on top of each chop. Cover chops with 4 remaining chops, pressing together lightly.
3. Sprinkle brown gravy mix over top of chops. (To make an even layer, sift mixture through a small strainer.
4. Cover with waxed paper and cook on 70 (roast) for 14 to 18 minutes, or just until done.

Orange Ginger Pork Chops

6 servings

6 lean pork chops
¼ cup orange juice
½ teaspoon salt

1 teaspoon ground ginger
1 large orange, peeled and sliced
Dairy sour cream

1. Trim fat from pork chops. Place in an oblong microproof baking dish. Pour orange juice over chops. Cover with waxed paper and cook on HI (max. power) for 10 minutes.
2. Remove from oven. Turn chops over. Sprinkle with salt and ginger. Place an orange slice on top of each chop. Cover and cook on HI (max. power) for 10 minutes.
3. Remove from oven. Top each chop with a spoonful of sour cream. Cover and let stand 5 minutes before serving.

Barbecued Spareribs *(Illustrated on page 51)*

4 servings

1 tablespoon cooking oil
¼ cup minced onions
1 can (8 ounces) tomato sauce
1 tablespoon lemon juice
1 tablespoon brown sugar
1½ teaspoons sugar

1 teaspoon Worcestershire sauce
½ teaspoon prepared mustard
½ teaspoon salt
⅛ teaspoon pepper
1½ pounds spareribs

1. Put oil and onion in a 2-quart glass measure. Cover with waxed paper and cook on HI (max. power) for 3 to 4 minutes.
2. Add 2 tablespoons water and remaining ingredients except spareribs. Stir. Cover and cook on HI (max. power) for 3 minutes. Let stand, covered.
3. Cut ribs apart between bones and place in a 3-quart microproof casserole. Cover and cook on 70 (roast) for 15 minutes.
4. Pour off fat and juices. Cover ribs with ¾ cup of the barbecue sauce mixture. Cook, uncovered, on 70 (roast) for 15 minutes.
5. Turn ribs over. Spoon remaining sauce over top. Cover with waxed paper and cook on 70 (roast) for 10 to 20 minutes, or until meat is done. Let stand 5 minutes before serving.

It's the sauce that makes these spareribs so special. You'll also want to use it on chicken or steak. The recipe provides about 1½ cups sauce

---

Baked Ham Steak

2 servings

1 precooked ham steak, about 1 pound

2 teaspoons brown sugar
½ teaspoon prepared mustard

1. Put ham steak in a microproof baking dish. Cover with waxed paper and cook on 70 (roast) for 4 minutes. Remove from oven. Drain and reserve juices.
2. Mix juices with brown sugar and mustard. Spread over top of steak. Cook, uncovered, on 70 (roast) for 2 minutes.
3. Cover loosely and let stand 2 or 3 minutes before serving.

Baked Ham

10 to 12 servings

1 precooked smoked ham, about 4 pounds
1 can (4 ounces) sliced pineapple

¼ cup brown sugar
Whole cloves

1. Place ham, fat side down, on a microwave roasting rack in a 12- x 7-inch microproof baking dish. Cook on 70 (roast) for 10 minutes.
2. Remove ham from oven. Turn fat side up. Drain pineapple; reserve juice. Combine 2 tablespoons of the pineapple juice with brown sugar to make a paste. Spread over top of ham. Put pineapple slices on top and stud with cloves. Insert temperature probe into thickest part of ham, making sure temperature probe does not touch the bone or a fat pocket. Cook on 70 (roast) set at 120°.
3. Let stand, covered with aluminum foil, about 10 minutes before carving.

Ham Casserole

4 servings

¾ cups uncooked narrow egg noodles
1½ cups diced cooked ham
2 tablespoons chopped onion
⅛ teaspoon tarragon
2 tablespoons butter or margarine

1 can (10½ ounces) condensed cream of chicken soup, undiluted
½ cup canned French-style green beans
2 tablespoons bread crumbs

1. Cook egg noodles according to chart on page 94. Set aside.
2. Combine ham, onion, tarragon, and butter in a 1½-quart microproof casserole. Cover and cook on HI (max. power) for 3 minutes.
3. Add chicken soup, egg noodles, green beans, and ½ cup water. Stir. Cover and cook on HI (max. power) for 5 minutes, or until hot. Stir once during cooking time.
4. Top with bread crumbs. Cover and let stand 2 to 3 minutes before serving.

Liver, Bacon, and Onions

4 servings

4 slices bacon	1 pound sliced beef liver
2 medium onions, sliced	Salt and pepper

1. Place bacon slices in a 10-inch microproof pie plate. Cover with paper towel and cook on HI (max. power) for 3 to 4 minutes, or until crisp.
2. Remove bacon; drain on paper toweling. Add onions to drippings, stir and turn onions to coat with drippings. Cover with paper towel and cook on HI (max. power) for 5 minutes, or until onion is transparent.
3. Move onions to the side of dish and add liver. Turn to coat both sides with drippings. Cover with waxed paper and cook on 70 (roast) for 8 to 10 minutes, or until no longer pink.
4. Season with salt and pepper. Serve liver topped with onions and crumbled bacon.

Bacon

8 strips

8 slices bacon

1. Separate bacon strips. Lay 4 slices in a microproof baking dish on 2 paper towels; cover with 1 paper towel. Lay 4 more slices on towel and cover with a final sheet of paper towel.
2. Cook on HI (max. power) for 5 to 8 minutes, or to the desired degree of crispness.

In cooking bacon in your microwave oven, a number of variables must be considered. Cooking time depends on the thickness of the slice, the amount of fat in the bacon, the number of slices being cooked, and the crispness desired. We recommend you use the quantity and method above as a test. Then, as you use your microwave oven, adjust as needed for the type and quantity of bacon being cooked. (Generally, lean slices require a bit more cooking time.)

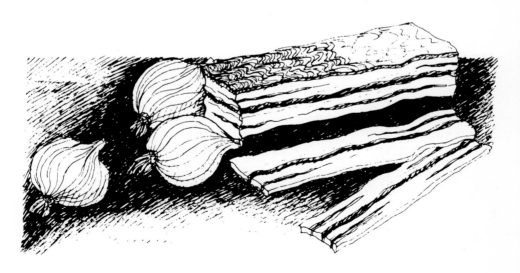

Veal Cordon Bleu

2 servings

½ pound veal round steak or cutlets,
  cut ½ inch thick
1 slice Swiss cheese
2 thin slices boiled ham
1½ tablespoons all-purpose flour

1 egg
¼ cup dry bread crumbs
1½ tablespoons butter or margarine
1 tablespoon chopped parsley
2 tablespoons dry vermouth

1. Cut veal into 4 pieces. Place each piece of veal between 2 sheets of waxed paper and pound with a smooth surfaced meat mallet until veal is ⅛-inch thick.
2. Cut cheese in 2 pieces. Fold each piece of cheese in half. Place on a slice of ham. Roll ham around cheese three times so that finished roll of ham is smaller than the pieces of veal. Place ham on 1 slice of veal and top with a second slice. Press edges of veal together to seal.
3. Put flour on a piece of waxed paper. Beat egg lightly with 1 tablespoon water. Put bread crumbs on a piece of waxed paper. Dip veal in flour, then in beaten egg, and finally coat well with bread crumbs.
4. Put butter and parsley in an 8-inch square microproof baking dish. Cook in oven for 1 minute, or just long enough to heat butter well.
5. Add veal to very hot butter. Cook, uncovered, on HI (max. power) for 4 minutes. Turn veal slices over after 2 minutes.
6. Pour wine over veal. Serve immediately.

Julienne of Veal

4 servings

1 pound boneless veal cutlet, about
  ½-inch thick
  Salt, paprika, and pepper
3 tablespoons butter or margarine,
  divided
2 tablespoons chopped green onion

¼ pound mushrooms, sliced
2 tablespoons all-purpose flour
¼ cup dry white wine
½ cup heavy cream
2 tablespoons brandy

1. Trim veal of all membrane. Place 1 piece of cutlet at a time between 2 pieces waxed paper. Pound with a smooth surfaced mallet or rolling pin until ¼ inch thick. Sprinkle meat lightly on each side with salt, paprika, and pepper. Cut into ¼-inch wide and 1½-inch long strips.
2. In 11- x 7-inch microproof baking dish, melt 2 tablespoons butter on 70 (roast) for 1½ minutes.
3. Stir in onion and mushrooms. Cook on HI (max. power) for 3 minutes; stir once during cooking time.
4. Add veal and cook on 70 (roast) for 5 minutes, or until no longer pink. Stir once during cooking time.
5. Lift meat and vegetables from drippings and set aside. Add remaining butter to baking dish and stir until melted. Stir in flour and cook on HI (max. power) for 1 minute.
6. Stir in veal drippings, wine, and cream. Cook, uncovered, on 70 (roast) for 3 minutes, or until smooth and thickened. Stir once during cooking time.
7. Add meat to sauce and cook, uncovered, on 80 (reheat) 2 minutes, or until completely hot. Remove from oven.
8. Put brandy in small microproof custard cup. Heat, uncovered, on 80 (reheat) 10 to 15 seconds. Remove, ignite, pour over meat and serve at once.

Veal Parmigiana

4 servings

1 egg
¼ teaspoon salt
3 tablespoons cracker crumbs
⅓ cup grated Parmesan cheese
1 pound veal cutlets
2 tablespoons cooking oil
¼ cup dry vermouth

1 medium onion, minced
1 cup (4 ounces) shredded
  mozzarella cheese
1 can (8 ounces) tomato sauce
⅛ teaspoon pepper
⅛ teaspoon oregano

1. Beat egg and salt in shallow dish. Combine cracker crumbs and Parmesan cheese on waxed paper square. Cut veal in 4 serving pieces; place between 2 pieces of waxed paper and pound with smooth surface of meat mallet until ¼ inch thick.
2. Preheat 9-inch square microwave browning dish according to manufacturer's directions. (Usually preheat 6 to 8 minutes and add cooking oil after preheating.)
3. Dip veal in egg then in cracker crumbs and brown 2 veal cutlets at a time in hot oil. Cover with waxed paper and cook on HI (max. power) for 1½ to 2 minutes. Turn and cook on HI (max. power) 1 to 1½ minutes. Remove and set aside. Brown second 2 cutlets in same manner.
4. Put all 4 cutlets in browning dish. Add vermouth, sprinkle onion over meat, top with cheese then sauce and season with pepper and oregano. Cover and cook on 60 (bake) for 10 minutes, or until sauce is hot and cheese melted.

Alternate method: If you do not have a browning dish, brown cutlets in skillet on top of stove. When brown, transfer to a 8- or 9-inch square microproof baking dish. Follow directions in Step 4. Use waxed paper to cover. Cook on 60 (bake) for 10 minutes. They are delicious!

POULTRY

Chicken, turkey, duck, and Cornish hen retain juices when cooked in a microwave oven. Because they require less attention than other meats, they are special favorites for microwave cooks on those days when too many things seem to be happening at once. Poultry turns out golden brown but not crispy brown. Experienced microwave cooks have found two tricks which you will be glad to know: If you have crisp-skin lovers at your table, you can keep them happy by crisping the skin in a conventional oven at 450°. The second surprise: Frustrations of long barbecue cooking can be avoided by partially cooking poultry first in the microwave oven, then finishing on the barbecue grill. Not a bit of the barbecue flavor is lost!

ADAPTING YOUR OWN RECIPES

It is extremely easy to adapt your conventional one-dish poultry recipes which call for cut-up pieces. Chances are, when the poultry is done your other ingredients will also be done. The temperature probe can help. Insert in thickest part of largest piece and set at 170°; cook on HI (max. power). Because ingredients and poultry pieces vary, a test for doneness is fork-tender meat. Tips:

- If stuffing is used, stuff poultry loosely just before cooking.

- Arrange poultry pieces in microproof baking dish with thickest side of poultry pieces toward outside of dish.
- If cooking legs, arrange in round microproof dish like spokes of a wheel, bony end toward center of dish.

USING THE DEFROSTING GUIDE

1. Poultry can be defrosted within the original paper or plastic wrapping. Remove all metal rings, twist ties, and wire. Remove any aluminum foil.
2. Place poultry in microproof dish while defrosting.
3. Defrost only as long as necessary. Poultry should be cool in the center when removed from the oven.
4. During standing time, poultry may be placed in a cold-water bath. While not required, it does aid defrosting.
5. Wing and leg tips and area near breast bone may begin cooking before center is thoroughly defrosted. Observe and cover such areas with small strips of aluminum foil if they appear thawed. Foil should be at least 1 inch from oven walls.

USING THE COOKING GUIDE

1. Defrost frozen poultry completely before cooking.
2. Remove the giblets; rinse poultry in cool water.
3. When cooking whole birds, place on a microwave roasting rack or an inverted microproof saucer in glass baking dish large enough to catch drippings.
4. Cook whole poultry covered loosely with waxed-paper tent to stop splatters. Toward end of cooking time, small pieces of aluminum foil may be used to cover legs, wing tips, or breast bone area to prevent overcooking. Foil should be at least 1 inch from oven walls.

5. Cover poultry pieces with either glass lid or plastic wrap during cooking and standing time.

6. Use temperature probe, inserted in thickest part of thigh, set at 180° for whole poultry and at 170° for parts, including turkey breasts. A common test for doneness in all poultry is when the meat cut near the bone is no longer pink. A regular meat thermometer can never be used in the microwave oven.

7. Standing time completes the cooking of poultry. Cover cooked whole birds with aluminum foil during standing time.

COOKING GUIDE—POULTRY

Poultry	First Setting and Time	Special Directions	Second Setting and Time	Meat Probe Setting	Minutes Standing Time
Turkey, whole: 8 to 14 pounds	HI (max. power) 5 minutes per pound	Start breast side down, turn over for second setting	70 (roast) 4 minutes per pound	180°	10 to 15
Turkey breast: 4 to 5 pounds	HI (max. power) 7 minutes per pound	Turn over	70 (roast) 5 minutes per pound	170°	10 to 15
Turkey parts: 2 to 3 pounds	70 (roast) 7 to 8 minutes per pound	Turn over	70 (roast) 7 to 8 minutes per pound	170°	5
Chicken, whole: 2 to 3 pounds	HI (max. power) 3 to 4 minutes per pound	Turn over	HI (Max. power) 3 to 4 minutes per pound	180°	5
3 to 5 pounds	HI (max. power) 4 minutes per pound	Turn over	HI (max. power) 4 minutes per pound	180°	5
Chicken, quartered: 2 to 3 pounds	HI (max. power) 3 to 4 minutes per pound	Turn over	HI (max. power) 3 to 4 minutes per pound	170°	5
Chicken, cut up: 1 to 2 pounds	HI (max. power) 3 to 4 minutes per pound	Turn over	HI (max. power) 3 to 4 minutes per pound	170°	5
Duckling: 4 to 5 pounds	70 (roast) 4 to 5 minutes per pound	Turn over and drain excess fat. For crisper skin, place duckling under conventional oven broiler before serving.	70 (roast) 4 to 5 minutes per pound	180°	8 to 10
Cornish hens: 1 to 1½ pounds each	(1) HI (max. power) 4 minutes per pound	Turn over	HI (max. power) 4 minutes per pound	180°	5
	(2) HI (max. power) 4 to 5 minutes per pound	Turn over	HI (max. power) 4 to 5 minutes per pound	180°	5

DEFROSTING GUIDE—POULTRY

Poultry	Minutes per pound	Setting	Minutes Standing Time	Special Notes
Turkey: 8 pounds and under Over 8 pounds	3 to 5 3 to 5	30 (defrost) 70 (roast)	60 60	Turn over once. Immerse in cold water during standing time.
Turkey breast: 4 pounds and under Over 4 pounds	3 to 5 1 2	30 (defrost) 70 (roast) 50 (simmer)	20 20	Begin 70 (roast); turn over, continue on 50 (simmer).
Turkey drumsticks	5 to 6	30 (defrost)	15 to 20	Turn every 5 minutes. Separate pieces when partially thawed.
Chicken, whole	6 to 8	30 (defrost)	20 to 25	Turn over once. Immerse in cold water during standing time.
Chicken, cut up	5 to 6	30 (defrost)	10 to 15	Turn every 5 minutes. Separate pieces when partially thawed.
Duckling	4	70 (roast)	20 to 30	Turn over once. Immerse in cold water during standing time.
Cornish hens: 1 to 1½ pounds each	(1) 12 to 15 (2) 20 to 25	30 (defrost) 30 (defrost)	20 20	Turn over once.

Product and Size	Container	Setting and Time	Special Notes
Precooked chicken: breaded pieces, frozen	Remove wrapping and place in microproof baking dish.	80 (reheat)	
1 piece		1 to 1½ minutes	
2 pieces		2 to 2½ minutes	
4 pieces		2½ to 3 minutes	
2 to 3 pounds, frozen		10 to 12 minutes	
Chicken Kiev: frozen	Remove plastic wrap and place on microproof plate.		Chicken Kiev needs two temperatures for best results.
1 piece		30 (defrost), 4 to 5 minutes HI (max. power), 2½ to 3 minutes	
2 pieces		30 (defrost), 6 to 7 minutes HI (max. power), 4 to 5 minutes	
Chicken Cordon Bleu: frozen	Remove plastic wrap and place top side down on microproof plate.		Cook on 30 (defrost). Turn top side up and continue cooking.
1 piece		30 (defrost), 4 to 5 minutes HI (max. power), 2½ to 3 minutes	
2 pieces		30 (defrost), 6 to 7 minutes (turn plate) 70 (roast), 4 minutes	
Chicken A La King: 5 ounces, frozen	Place on microproof plate.	HI (max. power), 3 to 4 minutes	Stir before serving.
Turkey Tetrazzini: 12 ounces, frozen	Place in microproof casserole or on microproof plate.	HI (max. power), 6 to 8 minutes	Stir halfway through cooking time.

Barbecued Chicken

4 servings

1 broiler-fryer chicken, 2½ pounds, quartered
½ cup bottled barbecue sauce
1 tablespoon parsley flakes
1 tablespoon onion flakes

1. Place chicken pieces, skin side up, with thick edges toward outside of a 12- x 7-inch microproof baking dish.
2. Combine remaining ingredients. Brush half of barbecue mixture over top of chicken. Cover with waxed paper and cook on HI (max. power) for 10 minutes.
3. Brush with remaining barbecue mixture. Cover and cook on HI (max. power) for 8 to 10 minutes, or until chicken is tender.
4. Let stand, covered, 5 minutes before serving.

Chicken Supreme
6 servings

5 slices bacon
1 can (10¾ ounces) cream of onion soup, undiluted
½ cup dry red wine or dry sherry
¼ cup instant minced onions
1 clove garlic, minced
1½ teaspoons instant chicken bouillon
1 tablespoon minced parsley
1 teaspoon salt

¼ teaspoon thyme
¼ teaspoon pepper
2 medium carrots, sliced thin
6 small new potatoes, peeled and halved
1 frying chicken, 2½ to 3 pounds, cut up
8 ounces fresh mushrooms

1. Cook bacon according to directions on page 56 until very crisp. Set aside.
2. Mix soup, wine, onion, garlic, bouillon, and seasonings in a small bowl. Put carrots and potatoes in bottom of 3-quart microproof casserole. Place chicken pieces on top, placing thicker portions around outside of dish and chicken wings in center. Pour soup mixture over the top.
3. Cover and cook on HI (max. power) for 30 minutes. Check vegetables and chicken for doneness. If necessary, rearrange chicken pieces, positioning vegetables in the center. Cook 1 to 2 minutes longer.
4. Add mushrooms and crumbled bacon on top. Cover and cook on 70 (roast) for 10 to 15 minutes.
5. Let stand 5 minutes before serving.

If your family prefers not to use wine, substitute water.

Cheesy Chicken
4 servings

¼ cup butter or margarine
¾ cup corn flake crumbs
⅓ cup grated Parmesan cheese
2 tablespoons chopped chives

2 tablespoons chopped parsley
1 broiler-fryer chicken, 3 pounds, cut in serving pieces

1. Place butter in an 8-inch square microproof baking dish. Cook on 70 (roast) for 1½ minutes, or until butter is melted.
2. Combine corn flake crumbs, cheese, chives, and parsley in a shallow dish. Dip pieces of chicken in butter and roll in crumb mixture.
3. Place chicken pieces in 8-inch square microproof baking dish, skin side up, with thickest pieces of chicken toward outside of dish. Cover with waxed paper and cook on HI (max. power) for 15 to 17 minutes, or until chicken is tender.
4. Let stand, covered, about 5 minutes before serving.

Quick Baked Chicken

4 servings

1 broiler-fryer chicken, 2½ to
  3 pounds
  Salt and pepper
1 small onion, quartered

2 stalks celery, cut in 1-inch slices
2 tablespoons soft butter or margarine
⅛ teaspoon thyme

1. Wash chicken. Remove giblets. Sprinkle inside of body cavity with salt and pepper. Place onion and celery inside body cavity. Tie legs together with string. Tie wings to body of chicken. Place chicken, breast side up, on a microwave roasting rack or inverted microproof saucer in a 12- x 7-inch microproof baking dish. Spread with soft butter and sprinkle with thyme.
2. Cook on HI (max. power) for 15 to 17 minutes or until done.
3. Let stand, covered with aluminum foil, about 5 minutes before serving.

Alternate method: To cook using the temperature probe, insert temperature probe in thickest part of thigh; cook on HI (max. power) set at 180°.

To help protect your oven from splatter, make a waxed-paper tent and place over chicken. If you're using the temperature probe, push it through the waxed paper and into the thigh.

Bacon-Flake Chicken

4 to 6 servings

5 slices bacon, cut in half
3 whole chicken breasts
1 cup milk

2 cups crushed corn flakes
  Salt and pepper
  Garlic salt

1. Put bacon in a shallow 8-inch square microproof baking dish. Cover with waxed paper and cook on HI (max. power) for 5 minutes.
2. Turn bacon over, cover, and cook on HI (max. power) for 3 minutes, or until very crisp; drain fat.
3. Cut chicken breasts in half. Remove skin and breastbone. Dip chicken in milk and roll in corn flakes. Pat corn flakes on so that they stick all over chicken. Place on top of cooked bacon. Pour remaining milk carefully into dish without disturbing chicken. Cook, uncovered, on HI (max. power) for 5 minutes.
4. Turn chicken over. Sprinkle with salt and pepper. Cook on 60 (bake) for 8 minutes. Let stand 3 minutes before serving. Sprinkle with garlic salt just before serving.

Chicken Cacciatore

5 to 6 servings

1 medium onion, chopped
1 medium green pepper, seeded and sliced thin
1 tablespoon butter or margarine
1 can (28 ounces) whole tomatoes
¼ cup all-purpose flour
1 bay leaf
1 tablespoon parsley flakes
1 teaspoon salt

1 clove garlic, minced
½ teaspoon oregano
1 teaspoon paprika
¼ teaspoon pepper
¼ teaspoon basil
½ cup dry red wine or water
1 frying chicken, 2½ to 3½ pounds, cut up

1. Put onion, green pepper, and butter in a 3-quart microproof casserole. Cover and cook on HI (max. power) for 9 to 10 minutes, or until onion is transparent.
2. Add tomatoes and flour; stir until smooth. Stir in all remaining ingredients except chicken. Cover and cook on HI (max. power) for 5 minutes.
3. Add chicken, immersing in sauce. Cover and cook on HI (max. power) for 25 to 30 minutes, or until chicken is tender. Stir once during cooking.
4. Allow to stand 5 minutes, covered, before serving with hot spaghetti or rice.

Cornish Hens for Two

2 servings

2 Cornish hens, 1 to 1½ pounds each
½ cup currant jelly

1 tablespoon dry sherry

1. Wash hens and set aside giblets. Tie legs together and tie wings to body with string. Place hens, breast side down, on a microwave roasting rack or inverted microproof saucer in a 12- x 7-inch microproof baking dish.
2. Put jelly and sherry in a 1-cup glass measure. Cook on HI (max. power) for 1 minute, or until jelly softens. Stir well.
3. Brush one-half of jelly mixture over hens. Cook on HI (max. power) for 15 minutes.
4. Turn hens breast side up. Brush with remaining jelly mixture. (If wings or legs are cooked and drying, cover with small pieces of aluminum foil.) Cook on HI (max. power) for 10 to 12 minutes, or until meat cut near bone is no longer pink.
5. Let stand, covered with aluminum foil, 5 minutes before serving.

Alternate method: the temperature probe may be used in Step 4. Insert the temperature probe in fleshy part of thigh. Cook on HI (max. power) set at 180°. To eliminate splatters, form a waxed-paper tent for hens.

What to do with the giblets? Many poultry recipes, of course, don't call for gravy. So, make a gravy using the giblets anyway. Freeze it for those times a gravy would be nice but you've bought chicken pieces without giblets!

Chicken Cacciatore

Roast Orange Duckling

4 servings

1 fresh or thawed frozen duckling,
  4 to 5 pounds
1 orange, peeled and cut in chunks

1 medium onion, quartered
½ cup orange marmalade

1. Wash duckling and set aside giblets. Place orange and onion pieces in body cavity of duckling. Secure neck skin flap with toothpicks or wooden skewers. Tie legs together and tie wings to body. Place duckling, breast side down, on a microwave roasting rack or inverted microproof saucer in a 12- x 7-inch microproof baking dish.
2. Put marmalade in a 1-cup glass measure. Cook on HI (max. power) for 1 minute. Spread one-half of warm marmalade on duckling. Cook on 70 (roast) for 20 minutes.
3. Remove from oven and drain off excess fat. Turn breast side up. Brush with remaining marmalade. Cover with waxed paper and cook on 70 (roast) for 15 to 20 minutes, or until meat near bone is no longer pink.
4. Let stand, covered with aluminum foil, 10 minutes before serving.

For a crisper skin, brown duckling in a conventional oven, preheated to 450°, for 8 to 10 minutes or until brown and crispy on all sides. Watch carefully as marmalade will brown quickly.

Turkey Tetrazzini

6 servings

4 ounces uncooked thin spaghetti
3 tablespoons butter or margarine
1 can (4 ounces) sliced mushrooms, drained
⅓ cup finely minced onion
3 tablespoons all-purpose flour
2 cups chicken broth or milk

½ cup light cream
¼ cup dry vermouth
1 teaspoon salt
  Dash white pepper
¾ cup grated Parmesan cheese, divided
2 cups diced cooked turkey

1. Cook spaghetti according to directions on page 94. Drain immediately and rinse in cold water to stop cooking. Reserve.
2. Place butter in a 3-quart microproof casserole. Add mushrooms and onions. Cover and cook on 90 (saute) for 3 to 4 minutes, or until onion is transparent.
3. Add flour and mix to form a smooth paste. Cover and cook on HI (max. power) for 30 seconds.
4. Stir in chicken broth, cream, vermouth, salt, pepper, and ¼ cup Parmesan cheese. Blend well. Cook, uncovered, on 70 (roast) for 4 to 5 minutes, or until mixture comes to a boil and thickens. Stir once during cooking period.
5. Add cooked spaghetti, turkey, and remainder of cheese. Stir carefully. Cover and cook on 60 (bake) for 8 to 9 minutes, or until hot.
6. Let stand, covered, for 5 minutes before serving.

No leftover turkey? No problem. This recipe works equally well with chicken or ham substituted for the turkey!

Turkey with Nut Stuffing

8 to 10 servings

1 cup butter or margarine, divided
½ cup salad oil
2 large onions, minced
4 stalks celery, minced
5 quarts day-old bread crumbs or ½-inch cubes
2 teaspoons poultry seasoning
¼ cup chopped parsley
2 teaspoons salt
1 cup coarsely chopped walnuts or pecans
1 fresh or thawed frozen turkey, 10 to 12 pounds

1. Place ½ cup butter and salad oil in a 1½-quart microproof casserole or baking dish. Add onions and celery. Cover and cook on 50 (simmer) for 5 to 6 minutes. Combine with bread crumbs, poultry seasoning, parsley, salt, and nuts. Stir lightly.
2. Wash completely thawed turkey. Stuff neck opening with part of the stuffing. Secure skin flap with strong toothpicks or wooden skewers. Stuff body cavity with remaining stuffing. Tie drumsticks together with strong string. Tie wings tightly to body with string.
3. Place turkey, breast side down, on microwave roasting rack on large microproof baking dish. Cook on HI (max. power) for 5 minutes per pound.
4. Drain fat from pan and turn turkey, breast side up, on rack. Place temperature probe in thickest part of thigh. Cook on 70 (roast) set at 180°. Let stand 10 to 15 minutes before carving.

If you like an extra-crisp skin, place cooked turkey in a conventional oven, preheated to 450°, for 10 to 15 minutes or until desired crispness is reached. To prevent splattering during microwave cooking, whole turkeys may be covered with a waxed-paper tent.

Turkey Divan

1 bunch (1 to 1½ pounds) broccoli
8 to 12 slices cooked turkey breast
¼ cup Parmesan cheese
¼ cup grated Gruyere cheese

Medium white sauce:
2 tablespoons butter or margarine
2 tablespoons flour
½ teaspoon salt
1 cup milk

1. Clean and split heavy stalks of broccoli lengthwise. Cook according to directions in chart on page 103.
2. Place cooked broccoli in 12- x 7-inch microproof baking dish with flowerets at ends of dish. Cover center with slices of turkey. Set aside.
3. To prepare sauce, put butter, flour, and salt in 4-cup glass measure. Cook on HI (max. power) for 2 minutes. Stir after 1 minute. Put milk in 2-cup glass measure. Cook on HI (max. power) for 1 minute.
4. Gradually add warm milk to butter-flour mixture until smooth. Cook on HI (max. power) for 3 to 4 minutes. While cooking, stir until thick and smooth.
5. Add cheeses to warm white sauce. Stir until blended. Pour over turkey and sprinkle with additional Parmesan. Cover with plastic wrap; pierce in 2 places and cook on 60 (bake) for 5 minutes, or until turkey is hot.

SEAFOOD

When microwaved, fish and shellfish are tender, delicious, moist, flavorful, flaky, and firm! If you have never really enjoyed fish, try it cooked by the microwave method. It is a great taste experience. If you've thought your microwave cooks fast, you'll now see it perform even faster. Fish is prepared at the last minute. So, when planning a fish meal, plan to have everything ready before starting to cook the fish. Even the standing time is short.

ADAPTING YOUR OWN RECIPES

Obviously, if the only way your family will eat seafood is when it is fried to a crackly-crisp, you won't be too impressed by the ease in adapting conventional recipes. Microwave cooking produces fish so delicious, as though it has been pampered and poached by the most famous French chef, that you just might coax some new seafood appetites to life. Use the charts as a guide for times. If you don't find something there, or in the recipes, that matches or comes close to the conventional recipe you want to adapt, begin by cooking at 70 (roast) or at HI (max. power) for one-fifth of the time the conventional recipe recommends. Observe, and if it appears to be done earlier, touch "Stop" and check. Continue cooking, if it is not done, ½ minute at a time. Some guides:

- Fresh fish fillets take about 1 minute less to cook than frozen fillets.

- When cooking whole fish, the dish is rotated one-quarter turn several times during the cooking process to help provide even cooking. The odd shape of the fish requires this procedure.
- Always cook seafood as soon after thawing as possible.
- Most recipes specifying a particular variety also work well when any white fish is substituted.
- If overcooked, seafood becomes dry and tough. Be conservative in estimating cooking times.

USING THE DEFROSTING GUIDE

1. Fish may be thawed in original wrappers. First discard any aluminum foil, metal rings, twist ties, or wire. Always cover and keep covered during standing time.
2. Place fish, in wrappings or carton, on microproof dish.
3. The 30 (defrost) setting is used for all seafood.

USING THE COOKING GUIDE

1. Defrost seafood fully before cooking.
2. Remove original wrappings. Rinse under cold running water.
3. Place seafood in microproof baking dish. Place thick edges of fillets and steaks, and thicker ends of shellfish, toward the outer edge of the dish. Overlap thin edges and roll uniformly thin pieces.
4. Cover dish with plastic wrap (or waxed paper should recipe specify).
5. Test often during the cooking period. Seafood overcooks very easily. Fish fillets and steaks are done when the thickest part just *begins* to flake. Shellfish are done when they begin to firm and have just changed to pink or light red.
6. Method and timing are the same for seafood in the shell and seafood without the shell.

COOKING GUIDE—SEAFOOD

Seafood	Time in Minutes	Setting	Standing Time in Minutes
Fish fillets			
1 pound	5 to 6	HI (max. power)	4 to 5
2 pounds	7 to 8	HI (max. power)	4 to 5
Lobster tails			
1 pound	7 to 8	HI (max. power)	3 to 4
Shrimp			
8 ounces	3 to 4	HI (max. power)	1 to 2
Whole fish			
1½ to 2 pounds	10 to 13	70 (roast)	4 to 5
Fish steaks			
1 pound	5 to 7	HI (max. power)	5 to 6
Crabmeat			
1 pound	8 to 9	HI (max. power)	4 to 5

DEFROSTING GUIDE—SEAFOOD

Fish	Time in Minutes	Setting	Standing time in Minutes	Special Notes
Fish fillets				
1 pound	8 to 10	30 (defrost)	5	Carefully separate fillets under cold running water.
Lobster tails				
1 pound	6 to 7	30 (defrost)	5	If two in a package, separate under cold running water. Turn over halfway through defrosting time.
Shrimp				
1 pound	5 to 6	30 (defrost)	5	Separate shrimp halfway through defrosting time.
Whole fish				
1½ to 2 pounds	13 to 14	30 (defrost)	5	Carefully rinse in cold water to finish defrosting.
Fish steaks				
1 pound	5 to 6	30 (defrost)	5	Carefully separate steaks under cold running water.
Oysters				
12 ounce can, frozen	4 to 5	30 (defrost)	5	Remove from can, place in microproof casserole. Should be cold when thawed. Separate with fork.

Product and Size	Container	Setting and Time	Special Notes
Fish patties, breaded, frozen	Microproof serving plate	80 (reheat)	
1		1 to 2 minutes	
2		3 to 4 minutes	
6		5 to 6 minutes	
Fish sticks, breaded, frozen	Microproof serving plate	80 (reheat)	
4		2 to 3 minutes	
8		3½ to 4½ minutes	
1 pound	Microproof baking dish	HI (max. power), 9 to 11 minutes	
Tuna casserole, 11-ounce package, frozen	Place in microproof casserole	HI (max. power), 6 to 8 minutes	Stir halfway through cooking time and just before serving.
Shrimp or crab newburg 6½-ounce package, frozen	Place pouch on microproof serving plate	HI (max. power), 4 to 6 minutes	Pierce pouch to vent. Mix halfway through cooking time and just before serving.

Fillet of Fish Almondine
4 servings

½ cup slivered almonds
½ cup butter or margarine
1 pound fresh or thawed frozen fish fillets
½ teaspoon salt
¼ teaspoon dill weed
⅛ teaspoon pepper
1 teaspoon chopped parsley
1 tablespoon lemon juice

1. Place almonds and butter in an 8-inch square microproof baking dish. Cook, uncovered, on HI (max. power) for 5 minutes, or until almonds and butter are golden brown. Remove almonds and set aside.
2. Put fish in dish with butter, turning to coat both sides. Sprinkle with salt, dill, pepper, parsley, and lemon juice. Roll fillets and leave in dish. Cover with waxed paper and cook on HI (max. power) for 4 minutes. Uncover; sprinkle almonds onto fish.
3. Cover and cook on HI (max. power) for 2 minutes, or until fish flakes easily when tested with a fork.
4. Let stand 1 to 2 minutes before serving. Garnish with lemon wedges, sprigs of parsley, and sprinkle with paprika.

Sole, flounder, or any other white fish may be used depending upon availability in your area.

Fish Fillets with Mushrooms

3 to 4 servings

1 pound fish fillets
2 tablespoons butter or margarine
2 green onions, thinly sliced
½ cup sliced fresh mushrooms

1 tomato, peeled and cut in pieces
½ teaspoon salt
½ teaspoon lemon juice
2 tablespoons dry white wine

1. Arrange fish fillets in a 12- x 7-inch microproof baking dish with the thick edges toward the outside of the dish. Dot with butter. Sprinkle remaining ingredients over top of fish.
2. Cover with waxed paper and cook on HI (max. power) for 5 minutes.
3. Let stand, covered, 5 minutes.

Poached Salmon Steaks

4 servings

⅓ cup dry white wine
2 peppercorns
1 lemon, sliced thin
1 bay leaf
1 teaspoon instant minced onion
1 teaspoon salt
4 salmon steaks, ½ inch thick

Sauce:
½ cup dairy sour cream
1 tablespoon minced parsley
1 teaspoon lemon juice
½ teaspoon dill weed
Pinch white pepper

1. Put 1½ cups hot water, wine, peppercorns, lemon, bay leaf, onion, and salt in 11- x 7-inch microproof baking dish. Cook on HI (max. power) for 5 minutes, or until it reaches a full boil.
2. Carefully place salmon in hot liquid. Cover with plastic wrap and cook on HI (max. power) for 1 minute. Let stand 5 minutes before serving.
3. To prepare sauce, put all ingredients in 2-cup glass measure. Mix well. Cook on 50 (simmer) for 3 to 4 minutes, or until hot.
4. Drain salmon. Serve with heated sauce.

Salmon, halibut, cod, swordfish, red snapper—steaks or fillets—this recipe makes any fish a special treat.

Salmon Loaf

6 to 8 servings

1 egg
½ cup milk
¼ cup melted butter
3 slices soft bread, cubed

½ teaspoon salt
2 cans (16 ounces each) red salmon,
   bone and skin removed

1. Beat egg slightly and mix with remaining ingredients, blend well. Pack firmly in greased 8- x 4- x 3-inch microproof loaf pan.
2. Cover with waxed paper and cook on 70 (roast) for 25 to 30 minutes, or until center of loaf is done.
3. Let stand, covered, 10 minutes before slicing.

Alternate method: The temperature probe may be used in Step 2. Insert temperature probe in center of loaf. Cook on 70 (roast) set at 150°.

Salmon Loaf is nice served with Lemon Butter Sauce.

Lemon Butter Sauce

⅔ cup

2 tablespoons lemon juice
½ cup butter or margarine

⅛ teaspoon salt
⅛ teaspoon white pepper

1. Place all ingredients in 2-cup glass measure. Cook, uncovered, on HI (max. power) for 1½ to 2 minutes, or until hot. Stir.
2. Serve with fish or vegetables.

Stuffed Bass

4 to 6 servings

1 whole bass, about 3
   pounds, cleaned
½ cup butter
½ cup finely chopped onion
½ cup chopped fresh mushrooms
¼ cup minced parsley

½ cup fine dry bread crumbs
1 egg, beaten
1 tablespoon lemon juice
1 teaspoon salt
⅛ teaspoon pepper

1. Wash fish in cold water and pat dry with paper towel, set aside.
2. Place butter in 2-quart microproof casserole. Cook on HI (max. power) for 45 seconds, or until melted. Stir in all remaining ingredients. Pack lightly into fish. Close with toothpicks.
3. Place fish in 12- x 8-inch microproof baking dish. Cover head and tail with aluminum foil. Cover dish with plastic wrap and vent by puncturing in 2 places. Cook on HI (max. power) for 16 to 18 minutes or until fish flakes easily.
4. Allow fish to stand for 5 minutes before serving.

Steamed Clams with Garlic Butter

4 servings

2 dozen clams (or mussels) in the shell
½ cup butter or margarine

1 clove garlic, minced
1 tablespoon chopped parsley
1½ teaspoons lemon juice

1. Scrub clams in water with stiff brush to remove all sand and grit. Discard all clams that are even slightly open. Set aside.
2. Place clams, 12 at a time, in a circle in a microproof pie plate or serving dish. Place clams with hinged side out. Cover with plastic wrap and cook on HI (max. power) for 3 minutes, or until shells pop open.
3. Remove all clams that opened, set aside. Cook unopened clams on HI (max. power) for 30 seconds more. Discard all those that do not open. Cook second dozen.
4. Put butter, garlic, parsley, and lemon juice in a small microproof serving bowl. Cook on HI (max. power) for 1 to 1½ minutes, or until butter is bubbling.
5. Serve clams. To eat, clams are removed from shell and dipped in hot butter.

Crab and Spinach Quiche

6 servings

1 9-inch pastry shell
1 package (6 ounces) frozen crabmeat
4 eggs
1 cup light cream
1 teaspoon prepared mustard

⅛ teaspoon nutmeg
¾ teaspoon salt
2 tablespoons dry sherry
½ package (10-ounce size) frozen chopped spinach, thawed
1½ cups shredded Swiss cheese

1. Cook pastry shell according to directions on page 140. Set aside.
2. In original package, thaw crabmeat on paper towel on 30 (defrost) for 3 to 4 minutes. Set aside.
3. In large bowl, beat eggs. Add cream, mustard, nutmeg, salt, and sherry. Mix well. Drain spinach. Add spinach, cheese, and crabmeat to egg mixture. Stir well.
4. Pour into prepared pastry shell. Cook on 60 (bake) for 30 to 35 minutes, or until nearly set in center. Rotate dish one-quarter turn at ten-minute intervals during cooking time. Let stand 5 minutes before serving.

To thaw only the amount of spinach required, wrap one-half of the package with aluminum foil. Set on paper towel and thaw on 30 (defrost) for 3 to 4 minutes. Remove thawed portion from package. Return frozen portion to freezer!

Lobster Tails

4 servings

4 frozen lobster tails (4 to 6 ounces each)
1 teaspoon lemon juice
¼ cup butter or margarine
¼ teaspoon grated lemon peel

1. Place frozen lobster tails in an 8-inch square microproof baking dish. Sprinkle with lemon juice. Cook on HI (max. power) for 4 minutes to thaw lobster.
2. Cut away soft shell-like surface on underside of tail with a sharp knife or scissors. Insert wooden skewers into each lobster tail to keep flat while cooking. Drain liquid and arrange lobster in dish, shell side down.
3. Combine butter and lemon peel in a small microproof custard cup. Cook on 70 (roast) for 30 seconds, or until butter is melted.
4. Brush tails with butter mixture. Cover with waxed paper and cook on HI (max. power) for 7 minutes, or until lobster meat is firm.
5. Serve hot with melted butter and lemon wedges.

Scallops Vermouth

4 servings

¼ cup butter or margarine
1 tablespoon minced onion
2 tablespoons all-purpose flour
1 can (4 ounces) sliced mushrooms, drained
¼ cup dry vermouth
½ teaspoon salt
⅛ teaspoon pepper
1 pound bay scallops
1 bay leaf
2 teaspoons lemon juice
½ cup light cream
1 egg yolk
1 tablespoon chopped parsley

1. Combine butter and onion in a 2-quart microproof casserole. Cook, uncovered, on HI (max. power) for 2 minutes.
2. Stir in flour and blend well. Add mushrooms, wine, salt, pepper, scallops, bay leaf, and lemon juice. Stir carefully. Cover and cook on HI (max. power) for 6 minutes, or until scallops are tender.
3. Remove bay leaf. Beat cream with egg yolk. Add some of the hot liquid carefully to egg and blend well. Stir egg mixture carefully into hot casserole. Stir well. Cover and cook on 60 (bake) for 5 minutes, stirring once during cooking period.
4. Sprinkle with parsley and serve.

Oysters Rockefeller

6 servings

36 large oysters in the shell
1 package (10 ounces) frozen chopped spinach
2 tablespoons butter or margarine
1 tablespoon minced onion
3 tablespoons snipped parsley
1 tablespoon Worcestershire sauce
½ teaspoon salt
¼ teaspoon cayenne pepper
1 cup light cream
Parmesan cheese

1. Carefully remove oysters from shells. Set aside. Select 36 shell halves; those which will sit level are best. Rinse well. Place, open side up, in two 12- x 7-inch microproof baking dishes. Set aside.
2. Put spinach in 1½-quart microproof casserole. Cover and cook on HI (max. power) for 8 to 9 minutes. Drain well. Place between paper toweling and squeeze dry. Mix spinach, butter, onion, parsley, Worcestershire, salt, pepper, and cream.
3. Spoon one-half of spinach mixture onto shells. Add one oyster to each shell. Top with remaining spinach mixture and a generous sprinkling of cheese.
4. Cover each baking dish with waxed paper. Place one dish on middle rack and one on bottom shelf of oven. Cook on 70 (roast) for 6 to 8 minutes until oysters are plump and edges curled. Reverse dishes after 3 minutes. Let stand 5 minutes before serving. Garnish with lemon wedges.

This recipe can be halved. Place one dish on the bottom shelf and cook at 70 (roast) for 5 minutes.

Scalloped Oysters

6 servings

½ cup butter
2 cups coarse saltine crumbs
½ teaspoon onion powder
⅛ teaspoon white pepper
½ teaspoon Worcestershire sauce
¼ cup minced celery
1 pint oysters, drained; reserve ¼ cup liquid
½ cup milk
Parsley

1. Put butter in 4-cup glass measure. Cook on HI (max. power) for 1 minute, or until melted. Stir in crumbs, onion powder, pepper, Worcestershire, and celery.
2. Spread one-third of mixture in a 2-quart buttered microproof casserole. Spread one-half of oysters over crumbs. Repeat layers and top with remaining crumb mixture. Pour mixed oyster liquid and milk over layers. Cover and cook on HI (max. power) for 15 minutes. Rotate dish one quarter turn once during cooking time.
3. Let stand 5 minutes, covered, before serving. Garnish with minced parsley.

Shrimp Chow Mein

5 to 6 servings

1 medium onion, chopped
1 cup sliced celery
1 green pepper, cut in thin strips
2 tablespoons butter or margarine
1 can (16 ounces) bean sprouts, drained
1 can (4 ounces) mushroom pieces, undrained

2 tablespoons chopped pimiento
8 to 10 ounces cooked cleaned shrimp
2 teaspoons instant chicken bouillon
3 tablespoons cornstarch
3 tablespoons soy sauce

1. Put onion, celery, green pepper, and butter in 2-quart microproof casserole. Cover and cook on HI (max. power) for 9 to 10 minutes, or until tender. Add bean sprouts, mushrooms, pimiento, and shrimp; set aside.
2. Put 1¾ cups water, bouillon, cornstarch, and soy sauce in 4-cup glass measure; mix well. Cook on HI (max. power) for 6 to 7 minutes, or until mixture boils and thickens. Stir twice during cooking. Stir into shrimp mixture.
3. Cover and cook on HI (max. power) for 5 to 7 minutes or until heated. Stir once during cooking. Serve with hot rice or chinese noodles.

Shrimp Creole

4 to 6 servings

4 green onions, sliced thin
¼ cup chopped celery
½ cup chopped green pepper
2 tablespoons butter or margarine
1 clove garlic, minced
1 can (16 ounces) whole tomatoes

1 can (6 ounces) tomato paste
1 teaspoon salt
2 teaspoons parsley flakes
¼ teaspoon cayenne pepper
1 package (10 ounces) frozen cooked shrimp

1. Put onion, celery, green pepper, butter, and garlic in a 2-quart microproof casserole. Cover and cook on HI (max. power) for 3 minutes, or until onions are transparent.
2. Stir in remaining ingredients. Cover and cook on 80 (reheat) for 5 minutes. Stir.
3. Cover and cook on 80 (reheat) for 6 to 7 minutes, or until hot.
4. Let stand, covered, for 5 minutes before serving over hot cooked rice.

Alternate method: The temperature probe may be used in Step 3. Cook on 80 (reheat) set at 150°.

Tuna Crunch

4 servings

1 cup thinly sliced celery
¼ cup chopped onion
2 tablespoons butter or margarine
1 can (7 ounces) tuna fish

1 can (10¾ ounces) cream of
  mushroom soup, undiluted
1 can (3 ounces) chow mein noodles
½ cup coarsely chopped cashews

1. Combine celery, onion, and butter in a 1-quart microproof casserole. Cook, uncovered, on HI (max. power) for 5 minutes, stirring once during cooking time.
2. Drain tuna and flake with fork. Add tuna, soup, two-thirds can of noodles, and cashews to onion mixture. Stir carefully. Cover and cook on HI (max. power) for 2 minutes.
3. Stir mixture lightly. Top with remaining noodles. Cook on HI (max. power) for 3 to 4 minutes, or until hot.

Tuna-Spinach Casserole

4 servings

1 package (10 ounces) raw spinach
1 can (7 ounces) tuna fish
1 can (4 ounces) sliced mushrooms
2 tablespoons lemon juice
3 tablespoons butter or margarine,
  divided

1 tablespoon minced onion
2 tablespoons all-purpose flour
½ teaspoon salt
⅛ teaspoon pepper
1 egg, lightly beaten

1. Rinse spinach in fresh, cold water. Drain well. Break in pieces, removing tough center stems. Put in a 2-quart microproof casserole. Cover and cook on HI (max. power) for 3 to 4 minutes, or until spinach is limp. Drain well and set aside.
2. Drain tuna and set aside. Drain mushrooms, reserving liquid. Put mushroom liquid in a 1-cup measure. Add lemon juice and enough water to make 1 cup of liquid.
3. Put 2 tablespoons of the butter in a 4-cup glass measure. Cook on HI (max. power) for 30 seconds, or until butter is melted. Add onion, flour, salt, and pepper. Cook, uncovered, on 60 (bake) for 1 minute.
4. Stir in mushroom liquid. Cook, uncovered, on 60 (bake) for 5 minutes, or until thick, stirring occasionally during cooking time.
5. Add a small amount of sauce to egg, beat well, and return to hot sauce. Stir mushrooms into sauce.
6. Put drained spinach in a 2- to 3-quart microproof casserole. Break tuna in big chunks and place over top of spinach. Pour sauce over top. Dot with remaining 1 tablespoon of butter. Cook, uncovered, on HI (max. power) for 4 minutes.
7. Let stand, covered with waxed paper, 3 to 5 minutes before serving.

EGGS AND CHEESE

From a simple omelet, to a fancy quiche or a hearty baked eggs and hash, the microwave oven can enliven breakfast, brunch or any meal. Eggs are usually cooked at 70 (roast) or 60 (bake). They must always be removed from the shell for microwave cooking; it's just not possible to cook hard-boiled eggs in a microwave oven. It's also good to pierce the yolk gently before cooking, just a bit, to help steam escape. Cheese cooks best at 70 (roast), and that makes the two foods perfect microwave partners.

ADAPTING YOUR OWN RECIPES

No special tricks are necessary to adapt conventional recipes that use cheese and/or eggs as primary ingredients to microwave use. Keep in mind that microwave egg and cheese cookery calls for delicacy. Better to undercook than overcook. You can always continue cooking for a bit more time.

Tips:

• Cheese cooks very quickly and just seconds can mean the difference between good results and a rubbery disaster.

• Be free to substitute different cheeses for those specified. Some cheeses have especially good melting qualities but all will cook well.

• Puffy omelets and true soufflés do not cook well by the microwave method.

• Fondues and sauces profit from occasional stirring during the cooking time.

USING THE COOKING GUIDES

1. Eggs should be at refrigerator temperature.

2. Eggs will continue to cook for a bit after removal from oven, so remove just before done.

3. Use care not to overcook eggs. They become tough and unappetizing when overcooked.

4. To scramble eggs, break eggs into a microproof bowl or 4-cup glass measure. Add milk or cream; beat with a fork. Add butter. Cover with waxed paper. Cook at 60 (bake) for time indicated in chart. Let stand 1 minute before serving.

5. To poach eggs, bring water to a boil with a pinch of salt and ¼ teaspoon vinegar at HI (max. power). Break egg carefully into hot water. Pierce yolk with toothpick. Cover with waxed paper. Cook at 50 (simmer) for time required in chart. Let stand, covered, 1 minute before serving.

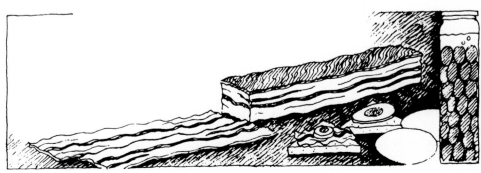

COOKING GUIDE—SCRAMBLED EGGS

Number of Eggs	Liquid	Butter	Minutes to Cook*
1	1 tablespoon	1 teaspoon	1 to 1½
2	2 tablespoons	2 teaspoons	2 to 2½
4	3 tablespoons	3 teaspoons	4½ to 5½
6	4 tablespoons	4 teaspoons	7 to 8

*For best results, stir eggs after two-thirds of cooking time has elapsed.

COOKING GUIDE—POACHED EGG

Number of Eggs	Water	Container	Minutes to Boil Water	Minutes to Cook
1	¼ cup	6-ounce microproof custard cup	1½ to 2	1
2	¼ cup	6-ounce microproof custard cups	2	1½ to 2
3	¼ cup	6-ounce microproof custard cups	2 to 2½	2 to 2½
4	1 cup	1-quart microproof	2½ to 3	2½ to 3

COOKING GUIDE—CONVENIENCE EGGS AND CHEESE

Product and Size	Container	Setting and Time	Special Notes
Soufflés: Corn: 12-ounce package, frozen	1½-quart microproof casserole, covered	HI (max. power), 10 to 12 minutes	Rotate casserole twice during cooking time.
Cheese: 12-ounce package, frozen	1½-quart microproof casserole, covered	HI (max. power), 11 to 13 minutes	Rotate casserole twice during cooking time.
Spinach: 12-ounce package, frozen	1½-quart microproof casserole, covered	HI (max. power), 12 to 15 minutes	Rotate casserole twice during cooking time.
Welsh Rabbit: 10-ounce package, frozen	1½-quart microproof casserole, covered	70 (roast), 6 to 7 minutes	Stir during cooking time.

Shirred Eggs

1 serving

1 teaspoon butter or margarine
2 eggs

1 tablespoon cream
Salt and pepper

1. Put butter in a microproof ramekin or small cereal bowl. Cook on 70 (roast) for 30 seconds to melt.
2. Break eggs carefully into ramekin. Pierce yolks carefully with toothpicks. Add cream. Cover tightly with plastic wrap and cook on 60 (bake) for 2 to 2½ minutes.
3. Remove and let stand 1 minute before serving. Season to taste.

Egg and Sausages

1 serving

2 precooked breakfast sausages
1 egg

1 tablespoon grated Parmesan cheese

1. Put 2 sausages in 4-inch microproof custard cups. Cover with paper towel and cook on HI (max. power) for 1 minute.
2. Pour off drippings. Break egg between sausages. Carefully pierce yolk with toothpick. Sprinkle top with cheese. Cover with waxed paper and cook on 70 (bake) for 1 minute, or until egg is almost set.
3. Let stand, covered, for 1 minute.

Omelet

1 to 2 servings

1 tablespoon butter or margarine
3 eggs
3 tablespoons water

½ teaspoon salt
⅛ teaspoon pepper

1. Place butter in a 9-inch microproof pie plate. Cook on HI (max. power) for 45 seconds, or until butter is melted.
2. Beat remaining ingredients lightly with a fork. Pour into pie plate. Cover with waxed paper and cook on 70 (roast) for 3 minutes. Stir lightly. Cover and cook on 60 (bake) for 1½ to 2 minutes, or until almost set in center.
3. Let stand, covered, 1 to 2 minutes before serving. Fold in half and serve.

Before folding omelet, top with crumbled cooked bacon, grated Cheddar cheese, chopped ham, or chopped tomato. Or, why not have your omelet go Western! Before cooking, add ¼ cup finely chopped cooked ham, 1 tablespoon finely chopped green onion, and 1 tablespoon minced onion.

Shirred Eggs with Sticky Buns (recipe, p. 154)

Cheesed Ham and Eggs

4 to 6 servings

¼ cup butter or margarine
¼ cup all-purpose flour
2 cups milk
1½ teaspoons prepared mustard
2 teaspoons Worcestershire sauce

1 cup shredded Cheddar cheese
1 cup diced cooked ham
6 hard-cooked eggs, peeled and
  halved
4 to 6 slices bread, toasted

1. Put butter in a 1½-quart microproof casserole or baking dish. Cook on HI (max. power) for 1 minute, or until melted. Blend in flour.
2. Put milk in 4-cup glass measure. Cook on HI (max. power) for 1 minute. Stir milk into flour mixture. Cook on 70 (roast) for 6 to 7 minutes, or until thickened.
3. Add mustard, Worcestershire, and cheese. Stir. Cook on 70 (roast) for 30 seconds, or until cheese is melted.
4. Stir in ham. Carefully fold in eggs. Cook on 70 (roast) for 1½ to 2 minutes, or until hot. Serve on toast.

Baked Eggs on Corned Beef Hash

2 servings

1 can (12 ounces) corned beef hash
2 eggs
2 tablespoons shredded Cheddar
  cheese

Salt
Pepper

1. Divide can of corned beef hash evenly between two 4-inch microproof custard cups. With the back of a spoon, make a hollow in the center of the hash. Break egg into the hollow. Pierce egg yolk carefully with a toothpick. Sprinkle each egg with 1 tablespoon cheese.
2. Cover with a paper towel and cook on 70 (roast) for 5 to 6 minutes, or until egg white is nearly opaque and hash is hot.
3. Let stand, covered, for 1 minute before serving.

Eggs Benedict

4 servings

¾ cup hollandaise sauce
2 English muffins, split and toasted

4 slices hams, ¼ inch thick
4 poached eggs

1. Prepare hollandaise sauce according to recipe below. Cover with a piece of waxed paper and set aside.
2. Place each muffin half on a paper towel lined microproof plate and top each with 1 slice ham. Cook, uncovered, two at a time, on 60 (bake) for 2 to 2½ minutes, or until ham is hot.
3. Top each with a poached egg prepared as instructed on page 85. Cover with hollandaise sauce and serve immediately.

Hollandaise Sauce

¾ cup

¼ cup butter or margarine
¼ cup light cream
2 egg yolks, well beaten

1 tablespoon lemon juice
½ teaspoon dry mustard
¼ teaspoon salt

1. Place butter in a 4-cup glass measure. Cook on HI (max. power) for 1 minute, or until butter is melted. Add remaining ingredients. Beat with an electric mixer until smooth.
2. Cook on 70 (roast) for 1 minute. Beat well every 15 seconds until thickened.
3. Remove from oven and beat with electric mixer until light and smooth.

If sauce curdles, beat in 1 teaspoon hot water and continue beating until mixture is smooth.

Cheese and Onion Quiche

6 servings

1 unbaked 9-inch pastry shell
4 slices bacon
1 small onion, sliced thin
1 tablespoon butter
1 cup shredded Swiss cheese
3 eggs

1 cup light cream
1 tablespoon all-purpose flour
½ teaspoon salt
⅛ teaspoon white pepper
¼ teaspoon dry mustard
  Paprika

1. Cook pastry shell according to directions on page 140. Set aside.
2. Cook bacon according to directions on page 56 until crisp. Set aside.
3. Put onion and butter in 4-cup glass measure and cook on HI (max. power) for 4 minutes, or until onion is transparent.
4. Spread cooked onion, crisp crumbled bacon, and cheese in pastry shell.
5. In 4-cup glass measure beat together eggs, cream, flour, salt, pepper, and mustard. Cook on 70 (roast) for 2 to 2½ minutes, or until slightly thickened. Stir twice during cooking.
6. Pour carefully over onion-bacon mixture. Cook on 70 (roast) for 10 to 11 minutes, or until nearly set in center. Rotate dish a quarter turn twice during cooking.
7. Sprinkle with paprika. Allow to stand 5 minutes (to finish cooking center) before serving.

Cheddar and Onion Egg

1 serving

1 teaspoon butter or margarine
1 green onion, sliced
1 egg

1 tablespoon shredded Cheddar cheese

1. In 4-inch microproof custard cup melt butter on HI (max. power) for 30 seconds.
2. Add sliced green onion and cook on HI (max. power) for 1½ minutes, or until transparent.
3. Break egg into cup and carefully pierce egg yolk with toothpick. Sprinkle cheese over egg. Cover with waxed paper and cook on 60 (bake) for 1 minute, or until almost set.
4. Let stand, covered, for 1 minute.

A special brunch! Serve Cheddar and Onion Egg with hash brown potatoes and Canadian bacon slices.

Welsh Rabbit on Toast

4 to 6 servings

4 teaspoons butter or margarine
4 cups shredded sharp Cheddar cheese
¾ teaspoon Worcestershire sauce
½ teaspoon salt
½ teaspoon paprika
¼ teaspoon dry mustard
¼ teaspoon cayenne
2 eggs, lightly beaten
1 cup flat beer or ale, at room temperature
Toasted French bread slices

1. Melt butter in a 2-quart microproof casserole on HI (max. power) for 1 minute.
2. Add cheese, Worcestershire, salt, paprika, dry mustard, and cayenne. Mix thoroughly. Cover and cook on 50 (simmer) for 6 minutes, stirring once during cooking time.
3. Stir a little of the hot cheese into beaten eggs. Slowly add beaten eggs to hot mixture and stir briskly. Gradually stir in beer and blend well. Cover and cook on 50 (simmer) for 3 minutes. Stir well.
4. Cover and cook on 50 (simmer) for 3 minutes. Remove from oven and beat briskly with a whisk to blend thoroughly.
5. Serve over crisp toasted French bread.

Welsh Rabbit becomes a hearty meal when served with crisp bacon slices and garnished with tomatoes.

Cheese Strata

4 servings

8 slices day-old bread
1 cup shredded Cheddar cheese
4 eggs
2 cups milk
¼ cup minced onions
½ teaspoon prepared mustard
1 teaspoon salt
⅛ teaspoon pepper
Paprika

1. Trim crusts from bread. Place 4 slices in bottom of an 8-inch square microproof baking dish. Cover with shredded cheese. Top with remaining 4 slices of bread.
2. Beat eggs. Add milk, onions, mustard, salt, and pepper. Mix. Pour over top of bread slices. Sprinkle with paprika and cover with plastic wrap. Let stand at least two hours or overnight in refrigerator.
3. Uncover and cook on 60 (bake) for 25 to 28 minutes, or until liquid is all absorbed and a knife inserted in center comes out clean. Let stand 3 minutes before serving.

This makes a perfect brunch dish as it may be prepared the night before. For a crunchy texture, sprinkle top with crushed corn flakes before baking as directed in Step 3.

Swiss Cheese Fondue

6 servings

4 cups shredded Swiss cheese
¼ cup all-purpose flour
¼ teaspoon salt
¼ teaspoon nutmeg

Dash pepper
2 cups dry white wine
2 tablespoons Kirsch
1 loaf French bread, cut into cubes

1. In a 1½-quart microproof casserole or baking dish, combine cheese, flour, salt, nutmeg, and pepper. Stir carefully to coat cheese with flour. Stir in wine. Cover and cook on 50 (simmer) for 6 minutes, stirring three times during cooking time. Stir well after removing from oven to finish melting cheese.
2. If cheese is not all melted, cover and cook on 50 (simmer) for 1 minute. Stir in Kirsch.
3. Serve immediately with cubes of French bread. Spear each cube of bread on a fondue fork; dip into fondue and eat immediately.

If fondue cools during eating time, rewarm on 50 (simmer) for 1 to 2 minutes.

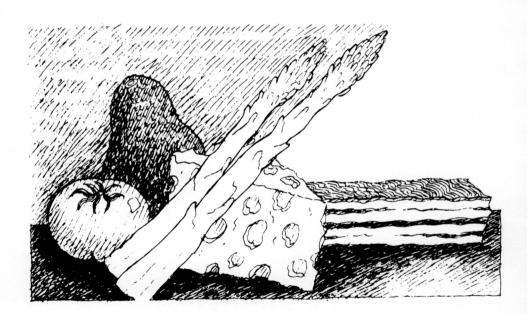

PASTA, RICE, CEREALS

This is one food grouping where the microwave oven really provides no significant time saving. It takes just as long to rehydrate these products in the microwave oven as it does conventionally. But the convenience in being able to cook and serve in the same dish, eliminating scorching and food stuck to pans, makes it well worthwhile. It is also great to know that you can reheat pasta, rice, and cereal without stirring or adding additional water. Finally, they are just as good reheated as when fresh cooked!

ADAPTING YOUR OWN RECIPES

You will probably find that your favorite rice- or noodle-based casserole can be easily adjusted, if necessary, to the volume used with one of the recipes here. Simply adapt your ingredients to the microwave method and follow the recommended microwave

cooking times, reduced by several minutes. Observe and extend cooking time in 1 minute intervals until done. Tips:

- If the pasta or rice is to be used in a casserole, it should be slightly firmer than if it is to be eaten at once. Simply cook a bit less.
- Quick-cooking rice may be substituted in converting from conventional recipes to assure the rice will cook in the short microwave cooking times.

USING THE COOKING GUIDES

1. After the water boils, normal cooking times are required for pastas and rice.
2. For pasta, combine water with 1 tablespoon salad oil and 1 to 2 teaspoons salt in microproof container. Bring water to a boil on HI (max. power). Stir. Cover. Cook at 50 (simmer) until done. Drain in colander, rinse in warm water. Serve.
3. For rice, add salt and margarine to water according to package directions. Bring water to full boil on HI (max. power). Stir in rice. Cover tightly. Cook on 50 (simmer) for time provided in chart. Let stand, covered, 5 minutes before serving.
4. For quick-cooking cereal, follow chart and package recommendations. Stir after removing from oven. Let stand about 1 minute before serving.

COOKING GUIDE—PASTA

Pasta	Covered Microproof Container	Water	Minutes to Boil Water	Amount of Pasta	Minutes to Cook
Spaghetti	3-quart casserole or baking dish	4 cups	8 to 10 on HI (max. power)	8 ounces	8 to 10 on 50 (simmer)
Macaroni	3-quart casserole	3 cups	8 to 10 on HI (max. power)	2 cups	10 to 12 on 50 (simmer)
Egg noodles	3-quart casserole	6 cups	10 to 12 on HI (max. power)	4 cups	14 to 15 on 50 (simmer)
Lasagna noodles	3-quart casserole or 13- x 9-inch baking dish	6 cups	10 to 12 on HI (max. power)	8 ounces	14 to 15 on 50 (simmer)
Spinach noodles	3-quart casserole	2½ cups	7 to 9 on HI (max. power)	1½ cups	9 to 11 on 50 (simmer)

COOKING GUIDE—RICE

Rice	Covered Microproof Container	Water	Minutes to Boil Water	Amount of Rice	Minutes to Cook
Short-grain white rice	2-quart	2 cups	4 to 5 on HI (max. power)	1 cup	13 to 15 on 50 (simmer)
Long-grain rice	2-quart	2 cups	4 to 5 on HI (max. power)	1 cup	15 to 17 on 50 (simmer)
Wild rice	3-quart	3 cups	6 to 7 on HI (max. power)	1 cup	35 to 40 on 50 (simmer)
Brown rice	3-quart	3 cups	6 to 7 on HI (max. power)	1 cup	40 on 50 (simmer)
Quick-cooking white rice	1-quart	1 cup	3 to 4 on HI (max. power)	1 cup	Let stand, covered, for 5 minutes, or until water is absorbed.

COOKING GUIDE—CEREAL

Servings	Water	Salt	Amount of Cereal	Minutes to Cook	Setting
1	¾ cup	¼ teaspoon	¼ or ⅓ cup, depending on cereal	2½ to 3	70 (roast)
2	¾ cup each	¼ teaspoon each	¼ to ⅓ cup each, depending on cereal	3½ to 4	70 (roast)

94

COOKING/DEFROSTING GUIDE—CONVENIENCE RICE AND PASTA

Product and Size	Container	Setting and Time	Special Notes
Rice			
1 cup cooked, refrigerated	Covered microproof dish or bowl	80 (reheat), ½ to 2 minutes	Let stand 2 minutes.
2 cups		80 (reheat), 3 to 4 minutes	
Pouch, 11-ounces, frozen	Microproof dish	80 (reheat), 6 to 7 minutes	Slit pouch before cooking. Let stand. Remove from pouch and stir lightly.
Fried rice, 10-ounce package, frozen	Covered microproof casserole	HI (max. power), 5 to 6 minutes	Stir twice during cooking time and before serving. Let stand 5 minutes.
Spanish rice, 12-ounce can	Covered microproof casserole	HI (max. power), 4 to 5 minutes	Stir twice during cooking time and before serving. Let stand 3 minutes.
Pasta			
Lasagna, 21-ounces frozen	Covered microproof casserole	70 (roast), 19 to 20 minutes	Let stand, covered, 5 minutes.
Spaghetti sauce, 32-ounces, canned	Covered microproof casserole	80 (reheat), 8 to 10 minutes	Stir during heating.
1 pint, frozen	Covered microproof casserole	30 (defrost), 1 to 2 minutes 80 (reheat), 6 to 8 minutes	Heat in container on 30 (defrost). Turn out into casserole. Cook on 80 (reheat). Stir and heat until hot.
Macaroni and beef, 11-ounce package, frozen	Covered microproof casserole	HI (max. power), 7 to 9 minutes	Stir twice during cooking time and before serving.
Macaroni and cheese, 10-ounce package, frozen	Covered microproof casserole	HI (max. power), 7 to 9 minutes	Stir twice during cooking time and before serving.
Spaghetti and meatballs, 14-ounce package, frozen	Covered microproof casserole	HI (max. power), 8 to 10 minutes	Stir twice during cooking time and before serving.

Macaroni and Cheese *(Illustrated on page 98)*   4 servings

1¼ cups uncooked macaroni
2 tablespoons butter or margarine
2 tablespoons all-purpose flour
¼ teaspoon salt
½ teaspoon Worcestershire sauce
½ teaspoon prepared mustard

⅛ teaspoon pepper
1 cup milk
2 cups shredded Cheddar cheese, divided
¼ cup cracker crumbs
Tomato wedges

1. Cook macaroni according to chart on page 94. Set aside.
2. Put butter in 4-cup glass measure and cook on HI (max. power) for 30 seconds, or until melted.
3. Stir in flour, salt, Worcestershire, mustard, and pepper. Put milk in 2-cup glass measure and cook on HI (max. power) for 1 minute, or until warm.
4. Gradually stir milk into flour mixture. Cook on HI (max. power) for 3 minutes. Stir once during cooking.
5. Stir. Cook on HI (max. power) for 1 minute, or until smooth and thickening. Stir in 1½ cups shredded cheese. Stir until melted.
6. Combine sauce and cooked macaroni in 1½-quart microproof casserole. Combine remaining cheese and cracker crumbs. Sprinkle over top of casserole. Cook on 60 (bake) for 5 to 6 minutes, or until mixture is bubbling.
7. Let stand, covered, for 5 minutes before serving. Garnish with tomato wedges, if desired.

Macaroni Supreme   8 to 10 servings

3 cups uncooked elbow macaroni
1 pound lean ground beef
1 large onion, finely chopped
1 can (35 ounces) Italian-style tomatoes
1 package (10 ounces) frozen peas
1 cup sliced fresh mushrooms

¾ cup dry red wine
¼ cup chopped parsley
1 teaspoon sugar
1 teaspoon salt
⅛ teaspoon pepper
2 cups grated Parmesan cheese, divided

1. Cook macaroni according to chart on page 94. Set aside.
2. Combine meat and onions in 2-quart microproof casserole or bowl. Cover and cook on HI (max. power) for 3 minutes. Stir. Cook on HI (max. power) for another 2 minutes, or until onion is transparent. Drain fat.
3. Add undrained tomatoes. With spoon, break up whole tomatoes into pieces. Add peas, mushrooms, wine, parsley, sugar, salt, and pepper. Cover and cook on 50 (simmer) for 30 minutes.
4. In 13- x 9-inch microproof baking dish, layer half the sauce, half of the cooked macaroni, and 1 cup cheese. Add remaining macaroni and sauce. Top with remaining cheese. Cover with waxed paper and cook on 60 (bake) for 10 to 12 minutes, or until cheese is melted and casserole is bubbling.
5. Let stand 5 minutes before serving.

Meatless Macaroni

8 servings

1 package (7 ounces) shell macaroni
3 tablespoons olive oil
1 large onion, sliced
2 cups sliced carrots
1 cup chopped celery
1 clove garlic, crushed
2 cups diced, peeled tomatoes
½ teaspoon sage
½ teaspoon oregano

¼ teaspoon pepper
¼ teaspoon ground basil
⅛ teaspoon thyme
⅛ teaspoon rosemary
2 cans (16 ounces each) kidney beans
Salt and pepper
Grated Parmesan cheese

1. Put 3 cups water in large microproof bowl. Cook on HI (max. power) for 8 to 10 minutes. Place macaroni shells in boiling water. Cover with waxed paper and cook on HI (max. power) for 1 minute. Let stand 5 minutes. Drain. Set aside.
2. Put oil in 3-quart microproof casserole. Cook on HI (max. power) for 2 minutes. Add onion, carrot, celery, and garlic. Continue cooking on HI (max. power) for 10 to 12 minutes or until vegetables are tender.
3. Add tomatoes and seasonings. Cover and cook on 70 (roast) for 7 minutes.
4. Add macaroni and beans. Cover and cook on HI (max. power) for 12 to 15 minutes. Stir. Cook on 70 (roast) for 18 to 20 minutes, stirring occasionally. Season with salt and pepper. Sprinkle with Parmesan cheese.

Try it this way: substitute ½ teaspoon cumin and ½ teaspoon chili powder for sage and oregano. Also substitute red pepper for black pepper, use chili (pinto) beans for kidney beans. Ole! Mexican Macaroni!

Spaghetti Sauce *(Illustrated on page 99)*

about 2 quarts

½ pound lean ground beef
½ cup chopped onion
2 cloves garlic, minced
1 can (28 ounces) tomatoes
2 cans (6 ounces each) tomato paste

2 teaspoons salt
2 teaspoons oregano
¼ teaspoon basil
¼ teaspoon ground thyme
⅛ teaspoon pepper

1. Crumble beef into a 3-quart microproof casserole. Add onion and garlic. Cook, uncovered, on HI (max. power) for 5 minutes. Stir to break up meat; drain off excess fat.
2. Add remaining ingredients. Cut tomatoes into pieces with spoon. Cover and cook on 50 (simmer) for 25 to 30 minutes, or until mixture is well blended and slightly thickened.
3. Cover and let stand about 5 minutes.
4. Serve over hot cooked spaghetti.

Following pages: Left, *Macaroni and Cheese* (recipe, p. 96); right, *Spaghetti Sauce* (recipe, p. 97)

Eggs and Noodle Casserole

6 servings

1½ cups uncooked spinach noodles
¼ cup butter or margarine
¼ cup all-purpose flour
1 teaspoon salt
¼ teaspoon hot-pepper sauce

2¼ cups milk
1 cup grated sharp Cheddar cheese
¼ cup grated Parmesan cheese
3 hard-cooked eggs, peeled and halved

1. Cook spinach noodles according to chart on page 94. Set aside.
2. Put butter in 1½-quart microproof mixing bowl. Cook on HI (max. power) for 30 seconds, or until melted.
3. Stir in flour, salt, and hot-pepper sauce to make a smooth paste. Cook on HI (max. power) for 30 seconds.
4. Put milk in 4-cup glass measure. Cook on HI (max. power) 2 minutes to warm.
5. Gradually stir milk into flour mixture. Cook on HI (max. power) for 4 to 5 minutes. Stir once during cooking time. Stir briskly to make smooth sauce. Add cheeses and stir until melted.
6. Put cooked noodles in 2-quart microproof casserole. Add cheese sauce and mix carefully. Cover and cook on 60 (bake) for 7 to 8 minutes, or until hot. Stir.
7. Top with egg halves. Cover and cook on 60 (bake) for 3 minutes. Let stand, covered, for 3 minutes before serving.

Chicken Noodle Casserole

4 to 6 servings

1½ cups uncooked broken narrow egg noodles
2 to 3 cups cut-up cooked chicken or turkey
1 cup chicken stock

½ cup milk
½ teaspoon salt
⅛ teaspoon pepper
1 cup shredded Cheddar cheese
¼ cup sliced stuffed green olives

1. In a 2-quart microproof casserole combine noodles, chicken, chicken stock, milk, salt, and pepper. Stir lightly.
2. Cover and cook on 70 (roast) for 8 to 10 minutes, stirring once, or until noodles are tender.
3. Stir in cheese and olives. Cover and cook on 20 (low) for 5 minutes, or until cheese is melted.

Spanish Rice

6 to 8 servings

1½ cups water
1 can (16 ounces) tomatoes
1 can (6 ounces) tomato paste
¼ cup finely chopped onion
1 teaspoon sugar

1 teaspoon salt
¼ cup chopped celery
½ teaspoon oregano
¼ teaspoon garlic powder
⅔ cup long-grain white rice

1. Combine all ingredients except rice in a 2-quart microproof casserole. Cover and cook on HI (max. power) for 5 minutes, or until boiling.
2. Stir in rice. Cover and cook on 50 (simmer) for 30 to 35 minutes, or until rice is tender.
3. Let stand, covered, 5 minutes before serving.

VEGETABLES

Your microwave oven enables you to enter one of the most exciting areas of the culinary arts. This is the world of delicious crisp-cooked vegetables. Because very little water is used, sometimes none at all, the loss of color, flavor, and nutrients is minimal. Even reheated fresh vegetables retain their original flavor and color. They do not dry out because the steam which heats them is primarily generated within the vegetables themselves. Of course, canned vegetables are better, too, because they can be drained before cooking, if desired.

ADAPTING YOUR OWN RECIPES

Vegetables are best when eaten still fairly crisp, in the oriental manner. However, if you prefer a softer texture in vegetables increase water and cooking time in the microwave recipe you choose to follow. Select one which is similar to the conventional recipe you wish to adapt. If your approach to vegetables has not been very creative in the past, use the extra time your microwave oven saves you to come up with a refreshing vegetable highlight for your next meal. Some tips:

- Whole vegetables with skins (squash, potatoes, etc.) must be pierced with a fork to allow steam to escape.
- Canned vegetables are best when cooked drained. The liquid can be reserved for use in soups.
- Freeze luncheon portions of your favorite vegetable dish in plastic pouches. Simply cut a steam vent in pouch and reheat on microproof plate.

USING THE COOKING GUIDE

1. All fresh or frozen vegetables are cooked and reheated on HI (max. power).
2. After cooking, allow all vegetables to stand, covered, for 2 to 3 minutes..
3. Add ¼-cup water for each ½ to 1-pound fresh vegetables. Don't add water for corn on the cob, squash, or baking potatoes.
4. Stir once during cooking time.
5. Pouches of frozen vegetables require steam vents. Slit pouch. Cook on microproof dish.
6. Frozen-in-sauce vegetables packaged in cartons rather than pouches are removed from carton and cooked in 1½-quart microproof casserole. Add liquid as package directs.

USING THE BLANCHING GUIDE

While microwaving is not recommended for canning, it can be a valuable and appreciated aid in preparing vegetables for the freezer. Some vegetables don't require any water at all and, of course, the less water used the better. You'll have "fresh picked" color and flavor for you produce. Some tips in preparing vegetables for blanching:

- Choose young, tender vegetables.
- Clean and prepare as for cooking.
- Measure amount(s) to be blanched; put, by batches, in microproof casserole.
- Add water, according to chart.
- Cover and cook on HI (max. power) for time indicated in chart.
- Stir vegetables half-way through cooking.
- Let vegetables stand, covered, for 1 minute after cooking.
- Put vegetables into ice water at once to stop cooking. When vegetables feel cool, spread on towel to absorb excess moisture.
- Package in freezer containers or pouches. Seal, label, date, and freeze quickly.

COOKING GUIDE—VEGETABLES

Vegetable	Amount	Approximate Cooking Time in Minutes	Fresh Vegetable Preparation
Artichokes: about 3½-inches in diameter	Fresh 1	4 to 5	Wash thoroughly. Cut tops off each leaf with sharp scissors. Cut 1 inch off top with a sharp knife.
	2	7 to 8	
	4	11 to 12	
	Frozen hearts, 10-ounce package	5 to 6	
Asparagus: spears and cut	Fresh, 1 pound	6 to 7	Wash thoroughly to remove sand. Snap off tough base and discard.
	Frozen, 10-ounce package	7 to 8	
Beans: green, wax and French cut	Fresh, 1 pound	12 to 14	Remove ends. Wash well and leave whole or break in pieces.
	Frozen, 9-ounce package	7 to 8	
Beets	4 medium, whole	16 to 18	Scrub beets. Leave 1 inch of top on beet. Peel and cut, or slice when beet is cooked.
Broccoli	Fresh, 1 to 1½ pounds	9 to 10	Remove tough outer leaves. Leave in stalks or cut stem in pieces and flowers in pieces.
	Frozen, 10-ounce package	8 to 10	
Brussel sprouts	Fresh, 1 pound	8 to 9	Remove outside leaves if wilted. Cut off stems. Wash.
	Frozen, 10-ounce package	6 to 7	
Cabbage	½ medium head, shredded	5 to 6	Remove outside wilted leaves.
Carrots	4 carrots, sliced	7 to 9	Peel and cut off tops. Slice, dice, or cut in slivers. Fresh young carrots cook best.
	6 carrots, sliced	9 to 10	
	8 tiny, whole	8 to 10	
	Frozen, 10-ounce package	8 to 9	
Cauliflower	1 medium, in flowerets	7 to 8	Wash and remove outside leaves.
	1 medium, whole	8 to 9	
	Frozen, 10-ounce package	8 to 9	
Celery	6 stalks, 1-inch slices	8 to 9	Clean stalks thoroughly.
Corn: kernel	Frozen, 10-ounce package	5 to 6	
Corn on cob	2 ears	4 to 5	Husk and wrap each ear in a square of waxed paper. Place on glass tray in oven, cooking no more than 4 at one time. Or, pull husks back three-quarters and remove silk. Tie husks closed with string. Arrange evenly in oven. Turn once during cooking time.
	4 ears	7 to 8	
	Frozen, 2 ears	6 to 8	
	Frozen, 4 ears	10 to 12	
Eggplant	1 medium, sliced	5 to 6	Wash and peel. Cut into slices or cubes. Pierce skin.
	1 medium, whole	6 to 7	

The microwave oven heats frozen foods perfectly.

COOKING GUIDE—VEGETABLES

Vegetable	Amount	Approximate Cooking Time in Minutes	Fresh Vegetable Preparation
Greens: collard, kale, mustard, etc.	Frozen, 10-ounce package	6 to 9	
Okra	½ pound Frozen, 10-ounce package	3 to 5 7 to 8	Wash thoroughly. Leave whole or cut in thick slices.
Onions	1 pound, equal size 1 pound, large and quartered	6 to 7 7 to 9	Peel. Leave whole. 1 tablespoon butter. Peel and cut. 1 tablespoon butter.
Parsnips	4 medium, quartered	8 to 9	Peel and cut.
Peas: green	Fresh, 1 pound Fresh, 2 pounds Frozen, 10-ounce package	7 to 8 8 to 9 5 to 6	Shell peas. Rinse well.
Peas: pods	Frozen, 6-ounce package	3 to 4	
Potatoes: sweet or yam	2 4 6	6 to 7 8 to 10 10 to 12	Wash and scrub well. Pierce with a fork all over. Place on paper towels, 1 inch apart.
Potatoes: white	1 whole 2 whole 4 whole	4 to 4½ 7 to 9 10 to 13	Wash and scrub well. Pierce with a fork all over. Place on paper towels, about 1 inch apart.
	9 quartered	12 to 16	To boil: Peel potatoes and cut in quarters. Place in microproof casserole. Add water, cover tightly, and cook.
Rutabaga	Fresh, 1 pound (4 cups)	9 to 11	Wash, peel and cube. ½ cup of water. 3 tablespoons butter.
Spinach	Fresh, 1 pound Frozen, 10-ounce package	6 to 7 7 to 8	Wash well. Remove tough stems or any wilted leaves. Drain.
Squash: acorn or butternut	1 medium, whole	10 to 12	Scrub and leave whole. Pierce with a fork in several spots. Cut and remove seeds to serve.
	cut, halves	8 to 10	Squash may be halved and placed, cut side down, on paper towels. Reverse for last minutes of cooking time.
Squash: zucchini	2 medium (3 cups)	7 to 8	Wash; do not peel. Cut in slices.

COOKING GUIDE—VEGETABLES

Vegetable	Amount	Approximate Cooking Time in Minutes	Fresh Vegetable Preparation
Succotash	Frozen, 10-ounce package	6 to 8	
Turnips	4 small, cubed (4 cups)	9 to 11	Peel. Wash and cut in cubes.
Vegetables: mixed	Frozen, 10-ounce package	7 to 8	

COOKING GUIDE—CANNED VEGETABLES

Canned Vegetables of All Kinds	Setting	Minutes Drained	Minutes Undrained	General Directions
8-ounces	80 (reheat)	1½ to 2	2 to 2½	Regardless of quantity: use a 4-cup microproof casserole; stir once while cooking. Let stand, covered, 2 to 3 minutes before serving.
15-ounces	80 (reheat)	2½ to 3	3 to 4	
17-ounces	80 (reheat)	3½ to 4	4 to 5	

COOKING GUIDE—CONVENIENCE VEGETABLES

Product and Size	Container	Setting and Time	Special Notes
Potatoes: au gratin, 11½-ounces, frozen	Microproof casserole. Cover with waxed paper.	70 (roast), 10 to 12 minutes	Let stand, covered, 3 minutes.
2 baked, stuffed, frozen	Microproof dish.	70 (roast), 10 to 12 minutes	Cover with waxed paper first.
Instant mashed	Covered microproof casserole.	HI (max. power), 5 to 6 minutes	Follow package directions for water, milk, butter, and salt. Reduce liquid by 1 tablespoon. When liquids are heated, add potatoes, whip with fork. Cover.
Spinach soufflé, 11½-ounces, frozen	Microproof casserole. Cover with waxed paper.	30 (defrost), 5 minutes 80 (reheat), 10 minutes	Let stand 3 minutes.

BLANCHING GUIDE — VEGETABLES *

Vegetables	Amount	Casserole Size	Water	Approximate Cooking Time in Minutes
Asparagus (cut in 1-inch pieces)	4 cups	1½-quart	¼ cup	4½
Beans: green or wax	1 pound	1½-quart	½ cup	5
Broccoli (cut in 2-inch pieces)	1 pound	1½-quart	⅓ cup	5½
Carrots (sliced)	1 pound	1½-quart	¼ cup	5
Cauliflower (cut in flowerets)	1 head	2-quart	⅓ cup	6
Corn* (cut from cob)	4 cups	1½-quart	none	4
Peas (shelled)	4 cups	1½-quart	¼ cup	4½
Spinach (washed)	1 pound	2-quart	none	4
Zucchini (sliced or cubed)	1 pound	1½-quart	¼ cup	4

*To quickly cool corn: set casserole in ice water; stir occasionally until cool.

*See Using the Blanching Guide on page 101.

Harvard Beets   4 servings

1 can (16 ounces) diced or sliced beets
¼ cup sugar
1 tablespoon cornstarch

½ teaspoon salt
⅛ teaspoon pepper
¼ cup vinegar

1. Drain beets, reserving liquid. Pour beet liquid into a 1-cup glass measure and add enough water to make 1 cup of liquid.
2. Combine sugar, cornstarch, salt, pepper, and vinegar in a 1-quart microproof casserole or bowl. Stir in beet liquid. Cook, uncovered, on HI (max. power) for 2 ½ to 3 minutes, stirring occasionally, until mixture thickens and is clear.
3. Add beets and stir lightly. Cover and cook on HI (max. power) for about 3 minutes, or until beets are hot.

Peppered Beans

3 to 4 servings

1 pound fresh green beans
2 tablespoons olive oil
½ sweet red or green pepper, seeded and cut in strips

¼ cup blanched slivered almonds
Salt and pepper

1. Cook beans according to directions on page 103. Cover and let stand.
2. Combine oil, red or green pepper, and almonds in a 1-quart microproof casserole. Cook, uncovered, on HI (max. power) for 3 to 4 minutes, or until peppers are limp.
3. Mix with green beans. Season to taste with salt and pepper.

Green Beans Italian

6 servings

3 slices bacon
2 packages (10 ounces each) frozen green beans

1 small onion, thinly sliced
¾ cup bottled Italian dressing

1. Cook bacon until crisp, according to directions on page 103.
2. Place green beans in 1½-quart microproof casserole. Cover and cook on HI (max. power) for 7 to 8 minutes, or until almost tender, stirring once during cooking time.
3. Add onions and Italian dressing. Cover and cook on HI (max. power) for 3 to 4 minutes, or until beans are crisp and tender and onion is transparent.
4. Serve hot with crumbled cooked bacon.

Super Green Beans

6 to 7 servings

4 tablespoons butter or margarine, divided
2 tablespoons all-purpose flour
1 tablespoon minced onion
¼ teaspoon salt
½ teaspoon grated lemon peel
¼ teaspoon pepper

1 cup dairy sour cream, room temperature
2 cans (16 ounces each) green beans, drained
½ cup dry bread crumbs
¼ cup grated Cheddar cheese

1. Put 2 tablespoons butter in 4-cup glass measure. Melt butter on HI (max. power) for 45 seconds.
2. Stir in flour, onion, salt, lemon peel, and pepper. Cook on HI (max. power) for 1 minute.
3. Stir in ¼-cup water. Stir in sour cream. Mix with green beans. Spoon into a 2-quart microproof casserole.
4. Put 2 remaining tablespoons butter in 2-cup glass measure. Cook on HI (max. power) for 30 seconds. Stir in bread crumbs and cheese; set aside.
5. Cook bean mixture, uncovered, on HI (max. power) for 5 minutes.
6. Sprinkle bread crumbs over beans. Cook on HI (max. power) for 2 minutes.

Creamy Broccoli-Carrot Casserole

5 to 6 servings

1 package (10 ounces) frozen broccoli
spears
1 can (10¾ ounces) cream of chicken
soup
½ cup dairy sour cream
1 cup finely shredded carrots

1 tablespoon all-purpose flour
1 tablespoon minced onions
¼ teaspoon salt
⅛ teaspoon pepper
2 tablespoons butter or margarine
¾ cup herb-seasoned stuffing cubes

1. Cook broccoli in package on paper towel at HI (max. power) for 2 minutes, or until you can separate spears. Set aside.
2. Put soup, sour cream, carrots, flour, onions, salt, and pepper in 1½-quart microproof casserole. Mix. Cut broccoli in one-inch pieces and stir into soup mixture. Cover and cook on HI (max. power) for 3 minutes. Stir carefully.
3. Put butter in 2-cup glass measure and cook on HI (max. power) for 1 minute, or until melted. Stir in stuffing and spoon over broccoli. Cook, uncovered, on HI (max. power) for 4 to 5 minutes, or until hot.

Cranberry Carrots

4 servings

1 package (10 ounces) frozen sliced
carrots
¼ cup butter or margarine

¼ cup jellied cranberry sauce
Salt

1. Cook carrots according to chart on page 103. Set aside.
2. Place butter in a 1½ to 2-quart microproof casserole. Cover and cook on HI (max. power) for 1 minute, or until butter is melted.
3. Add cranberry sauce. Cover and cook on HI (max. power) for 1 minute. Stir and cook until cranberry sauce is melted.
4. Add cooked carrots. Stir. Cook on HI (max. power) for 2 minutes. Season to taste.

Savory Cauliflower

6 servings

1 medium head cauliflower
½ cup mayonnaise or salad dressing
1 tablespoon instant minced onion
½ teaspoon dry mustard

¼ teaspoon salt
4 slices Colby cheese
Paprika

1. Cut cone shape wedge out of cauliflower core. Place cauliflower and ¼ cup water in 1½-quart microproof casserole. Cover and cook on HI (max. power) for 9 minutes. Drain.
2. Mix mayonnaise, onion, mustard, and salt. Spoon sauce over top of cauliflower. Lay cheese slices on top. Cook, uncovered, on 70 (roast) for 1 minute, or until cheese is melted. Sprinkle with paprika.
3. Let stand 2 minutes before serving.

Eggplant Parthenon

4 servings

2 medium eggplants
2 medium onions, chopped
1 pound ground lamb
1 beef bouillon cube
1 can (8 ounces) tomato sauce, divided
½ teaspoon oregano

¼ teaspoon cinnamon
2 tablespoons chopped parsley
½ teaspoon salt
¼ teaspoon pepper
½ cup dry bread crumbs

1. Wash eggplants and cut in half lengthwise. Scoop out insides, leaving a shell 1 inch thick. Chop eggplant pulp in medium chunks. Set aside.
2. Put onion in a 1½-quart microproof casserole. Crumble in lamb. Cover and cook on HI (max. power) for about 5 minutes, or just until lamb loses pink color. Drain fat.
3. Dissolve bouillon cube in ½ cup hot water. Stir into cooked lamb with ½ cup tomato sauce and the chopped eggplant pulp. Cover and cook on HI (max. power) for about 5 minutes, stirring occasionally.
4. Remove from oven; stir in oregano, cinnamon, parsley, salt, and pepper. Fill eggplant halves with mixture. Sprinkle bread crumbs over top. Drizzle remaining tomato sauce over top of crumbs.
5. Place eggplant halves in a 11- x 7-inch microproof baking dish. Cover with waxed paper and cook on 80 (reheat) for 8 minutes, or just until eggplant is tender.

Stuffed Green Peppers

8 servings

4 large green peppers
1 pound lean ground beef
1 medium onion, finely chopped
1 teaspoon salt

¼ teaspoon pepper
1½ cups cooked rice
1 can (8 ounces) tomato sauce, divided

1. Wash peppers. Cut in half lengthwise. Remove seeds and white membrane.
2. Crumble beef into a 1½-quart microproof casserole. Add onion. Cook, uncovered, on HI (max. power) for about 5 minutes, stirring once during cooking period. Cook until meat loses its red color, drain fat.
3. Stir in salt, pepper, rice, and ½ cup tomato sauce. Fill green pepper halves with mixture, mounding mixture on top. Place in a microproof baking dish. Top each pepper with remaining tomato sauce.
4. Cover with waxed paper and cook on HI (max. power) for 8 to 10 minutes, or just until peppers are tender.

Eggplant Parthenon, Stuffed Green Peppers,
Eggs in Nests (recipe, p. 112)

Eggs in Nests *(Illustrated on page 111)* 8 servings

8 small, firm-ripe tomatoes
¼ cup chopped parsley
¼ cup butter or margarine

1 large onion, chopped
8 eggs
Salt and pepper

1. Cut tops from tomatoes. Scoop out pulp and turn shells upside down on paper towels to drain. Discard seeds, chop pulp, and mix with parsley.
2. Combine butter and onion in a small microproof mixing bowl. Cover with paper towel and cook on HI (max. power) for about 4 minutes. Add parsley-tomato pulp mixture.
3. Stir mixture well and divide into tomato shells. Break 1 egg into each tomato shell, pierce yolk carefully with toothpick. Season lightly with salt and pepper.
4. Place tomatoes in an 8-inch square microproof baking dish. Cover with waxed paper and cook on 60 (bake) for 1 to 1½ minutes, or until eggs are set to desired degree of doneness.

Creamy Cabbage 5 to 6 servings

1 medium head cabbage
1 package (3 ounces) cream cheese, cubed
2 tablespoons milk
½ teaspoon salt

½ teaspoon celery seed
Dash pepper
Paprika

1. Shred cabbage into 2-quart microproof casserole. Add 2 tablespoons water. Cover and cook on HI (max. power) for 7 to 9 minutes, or until done. Stir once during cooking time.
2. Add all remaining ingredients except paprika. Cover and cook on HI (max. power) for 1 minute. Stir carefully to mix cheese with cabbage.
3. Garnish with paprika.

Red Cabbage Sweet and Sour 6 servings

1½ pounds red cabbage
1 tart apple, peeled, cored, and diced
1 tablespoon butter or margarine

5 tablespoons red wine vinegar
1 teaspoon salt
3 tablespoons sugar

1. Shred cabbage and put in a 3-quart microproof casserole. Add apple, butter, and vinegar. Stir. Cover and cook on HI (max. power) for 18 to 22 minutes, or until apples and cabbage are tender. Stir twice during cooking time.
2. Stir in salt and sugar. Cover and cook on HI (max. power) for 5 minutes, or until liquid boils.

Corn Pudding

4 servings

2 tablespoons butter or margarine
2 tablespoons all-purpose flour
1 can (16 ounces) whole kernel corn, drained

2 cups milk
2 eggs, well beaten
1 teaspoon salt
½ teaspoon pepper

1. Melt butter in a 1½-quart microproof casserole on HI (max. power) for 30 seconds.
2. Stir in flour to make a smooth paste. Add remaining ingredients and blend well.
3. Cover and cook on 70 (roast) for 10 minutes. Stir once during cooking period.
4. Let stand 10 minutes before serving.

For a hearty winter dinner, this dish goes well with ham or pork chops.

Sauteed Mushrooms

2 to 4 servings

½ pound fresh mushrooms
1 clove garlic, minced

⅓ cup butter or margarine

1. Clean mushrooms. Slice. Put in 8-inch microproof dish. Add garlic and butter. Cover with waxed paper and cook on 90 (saute) for 4 to 5 minutes.

Serve with roast beef or steak, or as a "surprise" side dish with any meal. Sauteed mushrooms also make an excellent main dish, served on toast, and sprinkled with Parmesan cheese!

Creamed Potato Bake

6 servings

1 package (16 ounces) frozen diced hash brown potatoes
1 can (10½ ounces) cream of potato soup
½ cup dairy sour cream

2 green onions, sliced
½ teaspoon salt
¼ teaspoon pepper
1 tablespoon minced parsley
Paprika

1. Put frozen potatoes in 1½-quart microproof casserole. Cover and cook on HI (max. power) for 5 minutes.
2. Stir in remaining ingredients except paprika. Cover and cook on 70 (roast) for 12 to 14 minutes.
3. Sprinkle with paprika. Cover and let stand for 5 minutes before serving.

Alternate method: The temperature probe may be used in Step 2. Cook on 70 (roast) set at 150°.

Scalloped Potatoes

4 to 6 servings

3 tablespoons butter
3 tablespoons all-purpose flour
1½ cups milk
¼ teaspoon salt

⅛ teaspoon pepper
3 cups sliced potatoes
1 small onion, sliced thin
Paprika

1. Melt butter in 4-cup glass measure, uncovered, on HI (max. power) for 1 minute. Stir in flour.
2. Heat milk in 2-cup glass measure, uncovered, on 70 (roast) for 2 minutes. Stir milk into flour mixture until smooth. Add salt and pepper.
3. Cook, uncovered, on 70 (roast) for 5 to 6 minutes or until mixture boils and thickens. Stir twice during cooking time.
4. In 2-quart microproof casserole, combine potatoes, onion, and white sauce. Cover with waxed paper and cook on 90 (saute) for 9 minutes. Stir.
5. Cover and cook on 90 (saute) for 9 to 10 minutes, or until potatoes are tender. Sprinkle with paprika.

Candied Sweet Potatoes

6 servings

6 medium sweet potatoes
1 cup brown sugar, firmly packed

2 tablespoons butter or margarine

1. Cook sweet potatoes according to chart on page 104. Peel and slice. Arrange in a 2-quart microproof casserole.
2. Combine sugar, butter, and ⅓ cup water in a 4-cup glass measure. Cook, uncovered, on 70 (roast) for 3 to 4 minutes, or until mixture is well blended and hot.
3. Pour over potatoes. Cover and cook on HI (max. power) for 7 to 8 minutes, or until heated through. Spoon glaze over potatoes occasionally while cooking.

Twice-Baked Potatoes

4 servings

4 baking potatoes
½ cup butter or margarine
½ cup dairy sour cream

½ teaspoon salt
Dash pepper
Paprika

1. Pierce potatoes and place on a paper towel, in oven, in a circle about 1 inch apart. Cook on HI (max. power) for 12 to 16 minutes. Potatoes may feel firm when done; let stand to soften. Do not overcook as potatoes will dehydrate.
2. Slice the top off each potato and, using teaspoon, remove centers to a mixing bowl. (Leave shells intact.) Add remaining ingredients. Mix with electric mixer until smooth. Divide mixture evenly in shells, mounding if necessary.
3. Place potatoes on microproof plate. Cook on HI (max. power) for 4 minutes. Sprinkle with paprika.

To prepare these potatoes ahead of time: cover and refrigerate after filling the shells. When you are ready, uncover, place on microproof plate, and cook on HI (max. power) for 6 minutes.

SANDWICHES

ADAPTING YOUR OWN RECIPES

On adapting your own recipes, all we need to say here is, "Yes!" Use several thin slices of meat. Thin slices heat more quickly and are better than one thick slice. The slower-heating thick slice often causes the bread to overcook before the meat is hot. Sandwiches may be placed on a paper plate, napkin, or paper towel to be warmed. Cover with a paper towel, also. Sometimes, with just one sandwich, it is convenient to wrap the sandwich in a paper towel which absorbs moisture. Remove wrapping immediately after warming. Already-baked frozen breads and rolls may be used for sandwiches. The filling, however, should be thawed first. Toasted bread is fine for sandwiches and provides a firm base. The toast is warmed only; no further browning occurs. Cook meat sandwiches, several thin slices of meat per sandwich, on HI (max. power) for :

1 sandwich	45 to 50 seconds
2 sandwiches	1 to 1½ minutes
4 sandwiches	2 to 2½ minutes

Sandwiches are a perfect example of how heating can enhance flavor. With your microwave oven, hot sandwiches are just seconds away. Sandwiches heat very quickly because, being porous, they have a low density. Since the filling is usually more dense than the bread or rolls, the filling determines the heating time. Surprisingly, the filling will always be hotter than the bread feels. Care must be taken not to overcook as the bread will become tough and chewy.

Sloppy Joe Sandwiches

6 servings

1 pound lean ground beef
½ cup chopped onion
½ cup chopped green pepper
½ teaspoon paprika
1 can (8 ounces) tomato sauce

1 teaspoon salt
Pinch sugar
Freshly ground pepper to taste
6 hamburger buns, toasted

1. Crumble beef in a 2-quart microproof casserole. Add onion, green pepper, and paprika. Cook, uncovered, on HI (max. power) for 4 minutes, or until meat loses its red color. Stir once during cooking time.
2. Break up meat with a fork and drain. Add remaining ingredients except buns and blend well. Cover and cook on HI (max. power) for 10 minutes, stirring twice during cooking time.
3. Spoon onto bottom half of toasted hamburger buns; cover with top half.

The Sloppy Joe mixture can be made well in advance and kept in the refrigerator. To serve, remove any congealed fat on top of mixture. Spoon desired amount of meat on hamburger buns or hard rolls, spreading mixture out to edges. Place single serving on a small paper plate. Cook on HI (max. power) for 1 to 1½ minutes, until mixture is hot.

Bermuda Grill

6 servings

2 cups chopped Bermuda onions	½ cup Sauterne
1 teaspoon salt	12 slices Swiss cheese
¼ teaspoon white pepper	12 slices rye bread, toasted

1. Place chopped onion in a shallow glass dish; sprinkle with salt and pepper. Add Sauterne. Cover and let stand at least 1 hour, stirring every 15 minutes; drain.
2. Place a slice of cheese on each of 6 toast slices.
3. Divide marinated onion over sandwiches and top with another slice of cheese, then a second slice of toast.
4. Place each sandwich on a paper plate or paper towel lined microproof plate. Cook one at a time on 80 (reheat) for 1 minute, or until cheese is melted.

Hot Salad Cheesewiches

4 servings

1 cup shredded Cheddar cheese	4 slices bread, toasted
½ cup diced cucumber	4 large thick tomato slices
1 tablespoon minced onion	8 slices dill pickle
¼ cup dairy sour cream	Paprika
⅛ teaspoon chili powder	

1. Combine cheese, cucumber, onion, sour cream, and chili powder.
2. Place each slice of bread on a paper plate or paper towel lined microproof plate.
3. Arrange a tomato slice and 2 pickle slices on each slice of bread. Divide the cheese mixture over the 4 slices, and sprinkle with paprika.
4. Cook each sandwich separately on 80 (reheat) for 1 to 1½ minutes, or until cheese melts and mixture is thoroughly heated.

Bacon Cheesewiches

6 servings

6 slices bacon	¼ cup catsup
1½ cups grated process American cheese	1 tablespoon prepared mustard
1 tablespoon instant minced onion	6 sandwich buns, split

1. Cook bacon according to directions on page 56 until crisp. Drain. Crumble bacon and combine with remaining ingredients except buns.
2. Spread 3 tablespoons bacon-cheese mixture on bottom half of each bun and cover with top. Wrap each sandwich in paper towel.
3. Cook 2 at a time on 80 (reheat) for 1 to 1½ minutes or until heated through. Serve hot.

Denver Sandwich

1 sandwich

1 egg
1 tablespoon minced onion
1 teaspoon minced green pepper

3 tablespoons diced ham
Toasted bun or 2 slices bread

1. Put all ingredients except bread in 1-cup glass measure; beat with fork. Pour into microproof saucer. Cook on 60 (bake) for 1 minute. Stir carefully.
2. Cook on 60 (bake) for 1 minute longer, or until set. Serve on toasted bun or bread.

Hot Ham 'n Swiss Rolls

6 servings

¼ cup butter or margarine
1 teaspoon prepared mustard
½ teaspoon onion powder
1 teaspoon poppy seed

6 large hard rolls, split
6 thin slices cooked ham
6 slices Swiss cheese

1. Blend butter, mustard, onion powder, and poppy seed in small bowl. Spread butter mixture inside each roll. Top with 1 slice each of ham and cheese. Cover with other half of roll.
2. Wrap each sandwich in paper towel or napkin. Place 2 at a time in oven. Cook on 80 (reheat) for 1½ minutes, or until rolls are hot.

Chicken and Ham Specials

8 servings

4 tablespoons butter or margarine
¼ cup all-purpose flour
1 teaspoon salt
⅛ teaspoon pepper
2 cups milk

3 tablespoons sherry
2 cups diced cooked chicken
8 slices baked ham
4 English muffins
Paprika

1. Put butter in 4-cup glass measure. Cook on HI (max. power) for 30 seconds, or until melted.
2. Stir in flour, salt, and pepper. Cook on HI (max. power) for 30 seconds.
3. Put milk in 2-cup glass measure and cook on HI (max. power) for 1 minute, or until warm.
4. Stir warm milk into flour mixture until smooth. Cook on HI (max. power) for 3 to 4 minutes. Stir twice during cooking.
5. Stir in sherry, chicken, and dash of paprika. Split English muffins and butter. Place 4 on paper towel lined microproof plate. Place 1 slice of ham on each muffin half. Divide chicken mixture over ham and sprinkle with paprika.
6. Cook 4 at a time on HI (max. power) for 2 minutes, or until heated through. Repeat with remaining muffin halves. Serve hot.

Reuben Sandwiches

4 servings

8 slices dark rye or pumpernickel
  bread
  Butter or margarine
½ pound thinly sliced corned beef

1 can (8 ounces) sauerkraut, drained
  Thousand Island dressing
4 slices Swiss cheese

1. Toast bread. Butter lightly.
2. Arrange sliced corned beef on 4 slices of toast. Divide sauerkraut among sandwiches. Top with Thousand Island dressing. Top each with a slice of Swiss cheese. Top with other slices of toast, buttered side down.
3. Place each sandwich on a paper plate or paper towel lined microproof plate.
4. Cook one at a time on 80 (reheat) for about 1 minute, or just until cheese is melted.

Barbecued Beef on a Bun

6 servings

¼ cup butter or margarine
1 pound top round steak
1½ tablespoons cornstarch
¼ cup beef broth
¼ cup lemon juice
½ cup chili sauce
1 tablespoon brown sugar
½ teaspoon salt

¼ teaspoon paprika
1 tablespoon Worcestershire sauce
1 small clove garlic, minced
1 teaspoon prepared horseradish
1 tablespoon instant minced onion
¼ teaspoon hot-pepper sauce
6 buns

1. Put butter in 2½-quart microproof casserole. Cook on HI (max. power) for 30 seconds, or until melted.
2. Cut round steak across grain in thin strips. Stir into melted butter to coat meat. Cover and cook on HI (max. power) for 4 to 5 minutes, or until meat is no longer pink. Stir twice during cooking.
3. Dissolve cornstarch in broth and lemon juice. Add to meat. Add all other ingredients, except buns. Stir. Cover and cook on HI (max. power) for 4 minutes. Stir once during cooking.
4. Let stand 2 minutes before serving. Serve beef strips and sauce in heated buns.

It's hard to imagine a sandwich that isn't improved by warming the rolls first. Six rolls are heated on 20 (low) for 2 to 3 minutes; four rolls take 1 to 1½ minutes.

Reuben Sandwich

Sausage and Pepper Heroes

(Illustrated on page 122)

4 servings

4 Italian sausages	4 hero rolls
½ cup prepared barbecue sauce	
1 green pepper, seeded and cut in strips	

1. Place sausages on microwave roasting rack   11- x 7-inch microproof baking dish. Cover with paper towels. Cook on HI (max. power) for 4 minutes. Turn sausages. Cook on HI (max. power) for 4 minutes longer. Drain fat. Set sausages aside.
2. Cook barbecue sauce with pepper strips in a 2-cup glass measure on HI (max. power) for 2 minutes.
3. Split hero rolls almost in half. Place 1 cooked sausage in each roll. Top with one-quarter of the sauce and peppers. Place each roll on paper towel on microproof plate. Cook, one at a time, on HI (max. power) for 1 to 1½ minutes, or until rolls are hot.

For party fun, make several batches. Place sausages and sauce with pepper strips in microproof casserole after Step 2. Refrigerate. Reheat using temperature probe inserted in center of casserole. Cook on HI (max. power) set at 150°. Have guests fill their own rolls. Cook, one at a time, on HI (max. power) for 1 to 1½ minutes, or until rolls are hot.

Hot Dogs *(Illustrated on page 122)*

1 serving

1 frankfurter roll	1 frankfurter
Prepared mustard	Pickle relish

1. Spread roll with mustard. Place hot dog in roll. Wrap in paper towel or napkin.
2. Cook 1 hot dog on HI (max. power) for 45 seconds. Cook 2 hot dogs at a time on HI (max. power) for 1 minute; cook 3 hot dogs on HI (max. power) for 1½ to 2 minutes; cook 4 hot dogs on HI (max. power) for 3 to 3½ minutes, or until hot. Serve hot with relish.

Cooking more than four hot dogs in buns at once is not recommended. The cooking time is so short, however, that cooking several batches should not be a problem.

Beans and Franks

6 servings

6 slices bacon, cut in eighths	1 can (16 ounces) pork and beans in tomato sauce
1 medium onion, chopped	6 slices toast
5 frankfurters, sliced	
1 tablespoon catsup	

1. Put bacon pieces in 1½-quart microproof casserole. Cover and cook on HI (max. power) for 2 to 3 minutes, or until cooked. Drain off all but about 1 table-spoon fat.
2. Add chopped onion. Stir. Cover and cook on HI (max. power) for 2 minutes, or until onion is transparent.

3. Add frankfurters. Stir. Cover and cook on HI (max. power) for 2 minutes.
4. Add catsup and beans. Mix well. Cover and cook on HI (max. power) for 4 minutes, or until hot. Stir once during cooking time.
5. Serve hot on toast.

Shrimp and Cheese Buns
6 servings

2 cups small cooked shrimp, chopped
¾ cup grated Swiss cheese
¼ cup sliced green onion
¼ teaspoon dill weed
2 tablespoons mayonnaise

1½ teaspoon vinegar
⅛ teaspoon salt
Dash pepper
6 hamburger buns, split, toasted, and buttered

1. Mix all ingredients together except buns. Spread mixture evenly and generously over bottom halves of buns. Cover with bun tops.
2. Wrap each sandwich loosely in paper towel or napkin. Cook on 80 (reheat) 2½ to 3 minutes (30 seconds per sandwich).

Cheeseburgers *(Illustrated on page 123)*
4 servings

1 pound lean ground beef
Salt and pepper

4 hamburger buns, split and toasted
4 slices process American cheese

1. Season ground beef to taste with salt and pepper. Shape into 4 patties. Place in an 8-inch square microproof baking dish. Cover with waxed paper and cook on 80 (reheat) for 2 minutes.
2. Turn patties over. Cover and cook on 80 (reheat) for 2 to 4 minutes to obtain desired degree of doneness.
3. Place 1 patty in each hamburger bun. Top patty with a slice of cheese. Place each Cheeseburger in bun on a small paper plate. Cook 1 or 2 at a time on 80 (reheat) for 1 minute, or until cheese melts.

The microwave browning dish or grill is a popular accessory. It gives hamburgers and other meats their familiar seared, browned appearance. If using your microwave browning dish for cheeseburgers, preheat dish on HI (max. power) for 6 minutes. Put patties in dish and cook on 80 (reheat) for 2 minutes. Then proceed as in Step 2, above.

Following pages: Left, *Sausage and Pepper Heroes, Hot Dogs* (recipes, p. 120); right, *Cheeseburgers* (recipe, p. 121)

Hot Swiss Tuna Buns

4 servings

1 can (6½ or 7 ounces) tuna fish, drained and flaked
½ cup finely shredded Swiss cheese
1 cup chopped celery
¼ cup mayonnaise

2 tablespoons catsup
1 teaspoon lemon juice
Salt and pepper
4 hamburger buns, split

1. Combine tuna, cheese, celery, mayonnaise, catsup, and lemon juice. Season to taste with salt and pepper. Divide tuna mixture among 4 buns.
2. Wrap each sandwich in paper towel or napkin. Cook 2 at a time on 80 (reheat) for 1 to 1½ minutes or until rolls are hot.

King Neptune Sandwiches

6 servings

1 can (6½ ounces) crabmeat, drained
1 can (4½ ounces) shrimp, drained
2 packages (3 ounces each) cream cheese
⅓ cup chopped almonds
2 tablespoons dry white wine
2 teaspoons lemon juice

1 teaspoon minced onion
1 teaspoon prepared horseradish
1 teaspoon prepared mustard
¼ teaspoon white pepper
½ teaspoon cayenne
6 French rolls
⅓ cup shredded Gruyere cheese

1. Pick over crabmeat and remove any cartilage, etc. Put cream cheese in 1½-quart microproof mixing bowl and cook on HI (max. power) for 1 minute to soften. Combine crabmeat and shrimp with cream cheese. Add almonds, wine, lemon juice, onion, horseradish, mustard, pepper, and cayenne.
2. Remove top third from each roll. Scoop out inside of bottom part being careful not to puncture shell. Spoon mixture evenly into 6 shells. Sprinkle cheese on top of filling. Place tops on rolls.
3. Place 2 rolls at a time on paper towel lined microproof plate. Cook on HI (max. power) for 1 to 1½ minutes, or until hot and cheese is melted. Repeat with remaining rolls.

HOT DRINKS

From breakfast cocoa to after-dinner coffee, your microwave oven will be busy performing at its best. What a convenience to stir up a cup of instant coffee, tea, or bouillon and heat it right in the serving cup! And it only takes a minute or two to heat. Coffee lovers will be happier, too. When you keep coffee warm, it deteriorates in 10 to 15 minutes. It soon becomes bitter. Now, brew your coffee as you normally do and pour what you want to drink now. Refrigerate the rest. Then, throughout the day, pour single cups as you wish direct from the refrigerator. Truly fresh coffee, once those single cups are heated in your microwave oven.

ADAPTING YOUR OWN RECIPES

Not much needs to be said here. Of course

you can heat any liquid in the microwave oven. Use care with milk-based drinks for they can boil over quickly. Fill cups just two-thirds full. You can use the temperature probe with any hot beverage, too. Set at 170° and cook on HI (max. power). Heat milk drinks on 70 (roast). Another tip of importance applies when heating several cups at once. Arrange in a circle and allow space between each for more even heating. Finally, you can use styrofoam, heavy plastic, and paper cups as well as microproof mugs or china cups (check china cups to be sure they do not have metallic trim).

USING THE COOKING GUIDE

1. Save time by making or reheating hot drinks right in the cup. Use glass or microproof mugs that have no silver or other metal trim.
2. Microwave water based drinks on HI (max. power).
3. Most beverages taste best if heated to a temperature of 170°.
4. Watch milk carefully so that it does not boil over. Heat on 70 (roast).
5. The temperature of the liquid before heating will make a difference in final heating time. Water from the cold tap or milk from the refrigerator will take longer to heat.

COOKING GUIDE—HOT DRINKS

Liquid	Setting	6-ounce Cup	Time in Minutes	8-ounce Cup	Time in Minutes	Special Notes
Water	HI (max. power)	1	1 to 1¼	1	1½ to 2	For instant
		2	1¾ to 2	2	3 to 3¼	coffee, soup, tea, etc.
Milk	70 (roast)	1	2½	1	2¾ to 3	For cocoa, etc.
		2	2¾ to 3	2	3¼ to 3½	
Reheating coffee	HI (max. power)	1	1 to 1½	1	1¼ to 1½	
		2	2 to 2¼	2	2 to 2½	

Hot Daiquiri

8 to 10 servings

¼ cup sugar
2 sticks cinnamon
8 whole cloves
1 can (6 ounces) frozen lemonade
   concentrate

1 can (6 ounces) frozen limeade
   concentrate
½ cup light rum

1. Combine 1½ cups hot water, sugar, spices, and concentrated fruit juices in a 2-quart microproof casserole. Cover and cook on HI (max. power) for 8 to 10 minutes, or until mixture boils.
2. Heat rum in a microproof container on HI (max. power) for 30 seconds. Ignite and pour over hot beverage. Ladle into punch cups for serving.

Russian Tea Mix

64 servings

1 jar (9 ounces) powdered orange
   breakfast drink
1 package (3 ounces) lemonade mix
¾ cup sugar
1½ cups instant tea

1 teaspoon cinnamon
¾ teaspoon ground ginger
1 teaspoon ground cloves
¼ teaspoon nutmeg

1. Mix above ingredients and store in covered jar or container until ready for use.
2. For 1 serving, place 1 or 2 teaspoons of above mix in microproof cup. Add water and cook on HI (max. power) for 1½ to 2 minutes.

West Coast Cocoa

4 servings

⅓ cup cocoa
⅓ cup sugar
3 cups milk

2 teaspoons grated orange rind
¼ teaspoon almond extract
Cinnamon sticks

1. Combine cocoa and sugar in 4-cup glass measure. Add ½ cup of milk to make a smooth paste. Stir in remaining milk, orange rind, and almond extract. Blend thoroughly.
2. Cook on HI (max. power) for 6 to 7 minutes until hot. Pour into mugs and garnish with cinnamon sticks.

Hot Buttered Rum

1 serving

4 teaspoons brown sugar
¼ cup light or dark rum
1½ teaspoons butter

Dash nutmeg
Cinnamon stick

1. Mix brown sugar and rum in tall microproof mug or cup. Add water to two-thirds full. Cook on HI (max. power) 1½ to 2 minutes until very hot but not boiling.
2. Add butter and sprinkle with nutmeg. Stir with cinnamon stick.

Clockwise from right: Hot Daiquiri, Russian Tea, West Coast Cocoa, Hot Buttered Rum, (recipes, above); Hot Cranberry Punch (recipe, p. 128)

Hot Cranberry Punch

16 half-cup servings

(Illustrated on page 127)

1 cup apple juice
3 cups cranberry juice
½ cup orange juice
3 tablespoons lemon juice
4 whole cloves

1 cinnamon stick
3 tablespoons sugar
1 orange, sliced
Whole cloves

1. Combine juices, spices, and sugar in a 2-quart microproof casserole. Cover and cook on HI (max. power) for 9 to 11 minutes or until mixture boils.
2. Strain into warmed punch bowl and garnish with clove-studded orange slices.

Holiday Eggnog

8 to 10 servings

4 eggs, separated
5 tablespoons sugar
½ teaspoon salt

½ cup sugar
3 cups milk
1 teaspoon vanilla extract

1. Beat egg whites until foamy. Gradually beat in 5 tablespoons sugar, 1 tablespoon at a time. Continue beating until stiff peaks form. Set aside.
2. Mix yolks, salt, and ½ cup sugar in microproof bowl and beat until thick and lemon colored. Stir in milk and vanilla. Cook on HI (max. power) for 8 to 9 minutes until hot, but not boiling, stirring occasionally.
3. Carefully fold in beaten egg whites. (Do not reheat eggnog after egg whites have been added as egg whites will cook.) Garnish with grated chocolate or a dash of nutmeg.

Irish Coffee

1 serving

3 tablespoons Irish whiskey
2 teaspoons sugar

1 tablespoon instant coffee
Whipping cream

1. Measure whiskey into an 8-ounce microproof glass or mug. Add sugar and coffee. Add water until container is three-fourths full. Mix well. Cook on HI (max. power) for 1½ to 2 minutes until hot but not boiling. Stir to dissolve sugar.
2. Whip cream until it is aerated but not stiff. Pour over a spoon onto the surface of the coffee without blending.
3. Do not stir. Coffee should be sipped through the layer of cream.

Cappuccino

4 servings

2 cups milk
4 teaspoons grated semi-sweet
  chocolate
4 teaspoons sugar

2 teaspoons instant coffee
4 ounces brandy
Whipped cream

1. Pour milk into 4-cup glass measure and cook on HI (max. power) for 3 to 3½ minutes or until hot but not boiling.
2. Stir in chocolate, sugar, and coffee until dissolved. Pour into 4 mugs.
3. Add 1 ounce brandy to each mug. Top with whipped cream. Serve warm.

Tomato Warmer

6 servings

2½ cups tomato juice
1 can (10½ ounces) condensed beef
broth
¼ cup lemon juice

1 teaspoon horseradish
1 teaspoon parsley flakes
½ teaspoon celery salt
4 tablespoons dry sherry

1. Combine all ingredients except sherry in a 4-quart microproof container. Cook on HI (max. power) for 8 to 9 minutes until hot, but not boiling.
2. Pour into 6 mugs and stir 2 teaspoons sherry into each mug.

FRUITS, PUDDINGS, PIES, SAUCES

Here are traditional family favorites, glamorous party desserts and spur-of-the-moment treats — all quick and easy with your microwave oven. This is a good spot to remind you about one of your oven's convenient special abilities: use your oven to soften and warm ready-made toppings and sauces for ice cream and cakes in their own glass jars (be sure to remove metal lids). Like vegetables, cooked fruit desserts will be newly-popular at your home because just-picked flavor is retained.

ADAPTING YOUR OWN RECIPES

Adapting conventional recipes in this category is a bit more of a challenge. Some pies seem to have a will of their own at times, though you can always expect good results with those which have very high sugar content. Some are more reliably produced if given a final 10- to 20-minute finishing in a conventional oven. Your pudding, sauce, and fruit recipes will convert to microwave methods easily and be extremely successful. Our tips:

- In sauces and fillings, use slightly less liquid than called for in the conventional recipe.
- Variety and ripeness of fruit will call for changes in the amount of sugar used and in cooking time. (Less sugar and less cooking time for ripe fruit.)
- For even cooking, select fruit of uniform size if to be cooked whole, as in baked apples.
- Remove baked custards from oven when centers are nearly firm. They will continue to cook and will set after removal.
- Do not overcook pudding. Overcooking causes pudding to thin while cooling.
- For better color and interesting flavor results, occasionally add 1 teaspoon cocoa or instant coffee mix to pie crust flour before mixing.
- All pies should be made in glass pie plates.

BAKING GUIDE—PIE CRUSTS

Pie Crust	Minutes to Cook	Setting	Special Notes
Unbaked pie crust	4 to 5	70 (roast)	Crust is done when surface appears flaky.
Box mix pie crust	4 to 5	70 (roast)	
Frozen, prepared pie crust	3 to 4	HI (max. power)	Remove from metal container and place in microproof pie plate.

BAKING GUIDE—PIES

Pie	Minutes to Cook	Setting	Special Notes
Fruit			
Fresh, 2-crust, 9-inch pie	8 to 10	HI (max. power)	After microwave cooking is completed, transfer to preheated conventional oven for 10 to 15 minutes at 450°.
Frozen, 9-inch pie	15	HI (max. power)	After microwave cooking is completed, transfer to preheated conventional oven for 10 to 15 minutes at 425°.
Custard			
Fresh, 1-crust 9-inch pie	30 to 35	50 (simmer)	Center should be nearly set.
Frozen, 1-crust, 9-inch pie	4 to 4½	70 (roast)	Center should be nearly set.

COOKING GUIDE—PUDDING AND PIE FILLING MIX

	Size of Package	Minutes to Cook (4-cup glass measure)	Setting
Pudding and pie filling mix, prepared per package directions	3¼-ounces, 4 servings	6½*	HI (max. power)
	5½-ounces, 6 servings	8 to 9	HI (max. power)
Golden egg custard	3 ounces, 4 servings	8 to 10	70 (roast)
Tapioca	3¼-ounces, 4 servings	5 to 7	70 (roast)

*Cook for 4½ minutes. Stir. Cook for 2 minutes.

Apricot-Orange Compote

6 servings

½ pound dried apricots
1 cup white raisins
Juice of 1 lemon, or 2 tablespoons lemon juice

½ cup sugar
1 can (11 ounces) mandarin oranges, drained

1. Rinse apricots and raisins in water. Drain. Put apricots and raisins in a 1½-quart microproof casserole. Add 1½ cups water and cook, uncovered, on HI (max. power) for 5 minutes.
2. Add lemon juice, sugar, and mandarin oranges. Cook on HI (max. power) for 5 minutes. Let stand 2 to 3 minutes before serving.

Baked Maple Bananas

4 servings

2 tablespoons butter or margarine
3 tablespoons maple syrup

4 bananas
Lemon juice

1. Place butter in a medium-size microproof baking dish. Cook on HI (max. power) for 30 seconds, or until butter is melted.
2. Add maple syrup. Mix. Place peeled bananas in dish. Coat well with butter mixture, using spoon. Cook on HI (max. power) for 1 minute.
3. Turn bananas. Cook on HI (max. power) for 1½ minutes. Sprinkle with lemon juice and serve warm.

Honeyed Blueberries

4 to 6 servings

3 cups bran flakes
½ cup honey
¼ cup sugar

1 teaspoon cinnamon
½ teaspoon nutmeg
2 cups fresh blueberries

1. In a bowl, combine bran flakes, honey, sugar, cinnamon, and nutmeg.
2. Grease an 8-inch square microproof baking dish. Spread half the bran flakes mixture on the bottom. Cover with half the blueberries. Cover blueberries with remaining bran flakes and top with remaining blueberries.
3. Cover with waxed paper and cook on HI (max. power) for 4 minutes. Serve hot.

Baked Grapefruit

4 servings

2 grapefruits
4 teaspoons dry sherry

4 teaspoons honey

1. Cut grapefruits in half. Loosen each section of grapefruit. Top each half with 1 teaspoon dry sherry and 1 teaspoon honey.
2. Cook on HI (max. power) for 5 minutes, or until grapefruits are very hot.

Baked Apple Supreme

6 servings

6 baking apples
Lemon juice
½ cup slivered almonds
¼ cup raisins

¼ cup brown sugar
2 teaspoons cinnamon
6 teaspoons butter or margarine

1. Wash apples and remove core, making a generous cavity in each apple. Remove thin circle of peel around cavity and sprinkle with lemon juice.
2. Mix together almonds, raisins, brown sugar, and cinnamon. Fill cavities with mixture and place each apple in a 3-inch microproof custard cup. Put 2 tablespoons of water in cup around apple. Dot each apple with 1 teaspoon butter. Cook on HI (max. power) for 10 minutes.
3. Let stand 3 minutes before serving.

Quick Applescotch

4 servings

1 can (16 ounces) pie-sliced apples
½ package (6-ounce size) butterscotch flavored morsels
1 tablespoon quick-cooking tapioca
½ tablespoon lemon juice

¼ cup all-purpose flour
¼ cup sugar
½ teaspoon cinnamon
¼ cup firm butter or margarine

1. Combine apples, butterscotch morsels, and tapioca in a 1-quart microproof casserole. Sprinkle lemon juice over the top.
2. Combine flour, sugar, and cinnamon in a small bowl. Cut in butter with a pastry blender or two knives until mixture resembles cornmeal. Sprinkle over top of apple mixture. Cook, uncovered, on 60 (bake) for 12 minutes, or until hot.
3. Serve warm with heavy cream or ice cream, if desired.

Cranberry-Apple Crunch

6 servings

1 cup sugar
2 cups chopped cranberries
2 cups chopped apples
1 cup quick-cooking rolled oats
½ cup firmly packed brown sugar

⅓ cup all-purpose flour
½ teaspoon salt
¼ cup butter or margarine
½ cup chopped nuts
Whipped cream

1. Combine sugar, 1 cup water, cranberries, and apples in a buttered 2-quart microproof casserole or baking dish. Cover and cook on HI (max. power) for 10 minutes.
2. In bowl, mix together oats, sugar, flour, and salt. Cut in butter with two knives to make a coarse mixture. Stir in nuts. Sprinkle over top of cranberry mixture. Cover and cook on HI (max. power) for 5 minutes.
3. Cook, uncovered, on HI (max. power) for 4 minutes, or until apples are done.
4. Let stand 3 to 4 minutes before serving. Serve with whipped cream.

Party-Pretty Pudding

8 servings

2 packages (3 ½ ounces each) pudding mix, vanilla flavored

2 pints fresh strawberries, hulled, sliced, and sweetened

1. Prepare pudding according to Pudding and Pie Filling Mix chart on page 131. Cool.
2. Spoon one-third of the cooled pudding into a serving dish. Cover with half the strawberries.
3. Repeat with a second layer of pudding and the remaining strawberries. Spoon the remaining third of the pudding on top of the strawberries.

For an even fancier treat, prepare layers in individual parfait glasses or serving dishes. Top with sweetened whipped cream.

Vanilla Mousse with Strawberry Sauce   8 to 10 servings

2 envelopes unflavored gelatin
1 cup sugar
1½ cups milk
2 eggs, separated
1 tablespoon vanilla extract
1 pint heavy cream, whipped

Strawberry sauce:
1 pint fresh strawberries
½ cup sugar
2 tablespoons cornstarch
½ cup lemon juice
2 tablespoons butter

1. Combine gelatin and 1 cup sugar in a large microproof mixing bowl and blend well. Stir in milk. Cook, uncovered, on HI (max. power) for 5 minutes, or until hot.
2. Beat egg yolks in a small dish. Gradually stir in a small amount of hot milk mixture. Add to large bowl of hot milk mixture. Blend well. Cook, uncovered, on 60 (bake) for about 4 minutes, or just until bubbles form around edge of bowl. Do not overcook or mixture will curdle.
3. Stir in vanilla. Place bowl in a pan or bowl of ice water. Cool until custard mounds when dropped from a spoon.
4. Beat egg whites until stiff but not dry. Fold into custard mixture. Fold in whipped cream. Turn mixture into a 2-quart mold. Chill in the refrigerator until set.
5. To make sauce: clean and hull berries. Reserve 1 cup of the best berries for garnish. Force the remainder through a food mill, or blend in an electric blender container. Put through a strainer to remove seeds.
6. Combine ½ cup sugar with cornstarch in a 1-quart microproof mixing bowl. Gradually stir in 1 cup water. Cook, uncovered, on HI (max. power) for 3 to 4 minutes, or until mixture comes to a boil and is clear. Stir once during cooking. Stir in lemon juice, butter, and strawberry puree. Chill sauce.
7. Unmold mousse on a serving platter. Garnish with whole strawberries. Serve with chilled Strawberry Sauce.

Old-Fashioned Indian Pudding

4 to 6 servings

2 cups milk, divided
¼ cup yellow cornmeal
2 tablespoons sugar
½ teaspoon salt
½ teaspoon cinnamon
¼ teaspoon ginger

1 egg, beaten
¼ cup molasses
1 tablespoon melted butter or margarine
Vanilla ice cream

1. Pour 1½ cups milk into a 1½-quart microproof casserole. Cook on 50 (simmer) for 5 minutes.
2. Combine cornmeal, sugar, salt, cinnamon, and ginger. Stir into hot milk. Cook, uncovered, on 50 (simmer) for 4 minutes. Stir well.
3. Beat together egg, molasses, and butter. Stir a small amount of hot milk mixture into egg mixture. Return to casserole. Stir well. Cook, uncovered, on 50 (simmer) for 6 minutes.
4. Pour remaining ½ cup cold milk carefully over top of pudding. Do not stir. Cook, uncovered, on 50 (simmer) for 3 minutes, or until set.
5. Let stand 10 to 15 minutes before serving. Serve warm, topped with vanilla ice cream.

Baked Custard

5 servings

1¾ cups milk
3 eggs
¼ cup sugar

¼ teaspoon salt
1 teaspoon vanilla extract
Ground nutmeg

1. Put milk into 1-quart bowl. Add eggs, sugar, salt, and vanilla. Beat with electric mixer until smooth. Pour equal amounts into five 6-ounce microproof custard cups. Sprinkle with nutmeg.
2. Arrange cups in circle in oven. Cook on 50 (simmer) for 9 to 12 minutes. Remove each custard cup as it begins to bubble or becomes almost set in center. Let stand 5 minutes before serving. Serve warm or cold.

Individual custards cook at different rates. Rather than rotate them as frequently as needed for a uniform cooking time, remove them from the oven as they become done. As you remove a custard, rearrange the remaining custards in the circle pattern.

Fresh Rhubarb Betty

6 to 8 servings

6 cups diced fresh rhubarb
1¼ cups sugar
2½ tablespoons quick-cooking tapioca
1 teaspoon grated lemon peel

1 tablespoon grated orange peel
⅓ cup butter or margarine
2¾ cups soft bread cubes
1 teaspoon vanilla extract

1. Combine rhubarb, sugar, tapioca, lemon peel, and orange peel in a bowl. Set aside.

2. Place butter in a 1-cup glass measure. Cover with waxed paper and cook on HI (max. power) for 45 seconds, or until butter melts. Pour butter over bread cubes in small bowl. Add vanilla and mix lightly.
3. In a 1½-quart microproof casserole, make alternate layers of rhubarb and bread cube mixture, ending with buttered bread cubes. Cover and cook on HI (max. power) for 5 minutes, or until rhubarb is cooked.
4. Serve warm or chilled.

Quick Peach Delight   4 servings

4 large canned peach halves	4 teaspoons brown sugar
1¼ teaspoons butter or margarine	Vanilla ice cream

1. Drain peaches thoroughly. Place in a 1-quart microproof baking dish. Put ¼ teaspoon butter in center of each peach. Sprinkle 1 teaspoon brown sugar on each peach half. Bake, uncovered, on HI (max. power) for 3 minutes, or until hot.
2. Serve warm with a small scoop of ice cream in center of each peach half.

Hot Fruit Salad   6 to 8 servings

¼ cup butter	2 cans (29 ounces each) fruits for salad,
⅔ cup brown sugar	drained
2 teaspoons curry powder	

1. Put butter in 2-quart microproof casserole. Cook on HI (max. power) for 1 minute, or until melted.
2. Stir in brown sugar and curry. Cook on HI (max. power) for 1 minute. Stir.
3. Add well-drained fruit and stir carefully to coat fruit. Cover and cook on 80 (reheat) for 8 minutes. Stir once during cooking. Serve warm.

Delicious served with lamb, pork, ham, or chicken.

Lemon Pineapple Creme   5 to 6 servings

¾ cup sugar, divided	2 tablespoons lemon juice
3 tablespoons cornstarch	2 eggs, separated
1 can (8 ounces) crushed pineapple, undrained	1 package (3 ounces) cream cheese, cubed
1 teaspoon grated lemon peel	

1. Mix ½ cup sugar, cornstarch, pineapple, and ⅔ cup water in 4-cup glass measure. Cook, uncovered, on HI (max. power) for 4 to 5 minutes, or until mixture boils. Stir twice during cooking time.
2. Stir in lemon peel, juice, and beaten egg yolks, then stir in cream cheese. Cook, uncovered, on 80 (reheat) for 1 minute.
3. Beat with electric mixer to blend in cream cheese. Cool.
4. Beat egg whites until frothy and gradually add ¼ cup sugar until soft peaks form. Fold into cooled pudding. Spoon into dessert dishes and refrigerate until served.

Cherry Cheese Pie

6 servings

1 baked 9-inch crumb crust
1 package (8 ounces) cream cheese
⅓ cup sugar
1 egg, beaten
¼ cup dairy sour cream
¾ teaspoon vanilla extract

Topping:
¾ cup dairy sour cream
2 tablespoons sugar
1 teaspoon vanilla extract
1 can (21 ounces) prepared cherry pie filling

1. Cook crumb crust according to directions below. Set aside.
2. In 1-quart microproof mixing bowl, soften cream cheese by cooking on HI (max. power) for 1 to 1½ minutes. Add sugar. Beat well. Add egg, sour cream, and vanilla. Beat until light and fluffy. Pour into prepared crust. Cook on 80 (reheat) for 4 minutes. Remove from oven and cool at least 8 minutes on cooling rack.
4. Prepare topping. Beat together sour cream, sugar, and vanilla. Spoon carefully over top of cooked cheese mixture. Cook on 80 (reheat) for 4 minutes, or just until set.
5. Spoon cherry pie filling around edge of pie. Chill thoroughly in refrigerator before serving.

Crumb Crust

1   9-inch pie shell

5 tablespoons butter or margarine
1 cup cracker crumbs

1 tablespoon sugar

1. Put butter in 9-inch microproof pie plate. Cook on HI (max. power) for 1 minute, or until melted.
2. Stir in crumbs and sugar; mix well. Press into bottom and sides of pie plate. Cook on 70 (roast) for 1 to 1½ minutes, or until set. Cool before filling.

To make a crumb crust, you can use, for example, graham crackers, chocolate wafers, gingersnaps, or vanilla wafers. If using fine crumbs rather than coarse, you may want to increase the amount to 1¼ cups.

Homemade Pastry

2 9-inch shells
or 1 double-crust pastry

2 cups flour
½ teaspoon salt

⅔ cup butter or margarine
4 to 6 tablespoons ice water

1. Put flour and salt in medium bowl. Mix. Cut in butter or margarine until mixture forms coarse crumbs. Sprinkle with water while mixing lightly. Form into ball.
2. Divide dough in half. On lightly floured surface, roll out each half to a 12-inch circle. If preparing two shells, place pastry into two 9-inch glass pie plates. Trim and flute edges. Prick pastry with fork. Cook each shell separately at HI (max. power) for 6 to 7 minutes.

To improve pastry color, add 1 to 2 drops of yellow food coloring to ice water. Or, brush diluted dark corn syrup on pastry before cooking.

Apple Pie

6 servings

1 double-crust unbaked pastry shell
7 medium cooking apples
¾ cup sugar
2 tablespoons all-purpose flour

⅛ teaspoon salt
1 teaspoon cinnamon
¼ teaspoon nutmeg
2 tablespoons butter

1. Prepare pastry dough according to directions above. Place one crust in bottom of 9-inch glass pie plate. Trim, prick crust, and set aside. Reserve second crust.
2. Pare, core, and slice apples (should make 6 cups). Put apples in large bowl. Add sugar, flour, salt, cinnamon, and nutmeg. Mix well. Pour apple mixture into unbaked shell.
3. Fit remaining crust over apples. Seal and flute edges; cut slits in top crust. Or, cut crust into strips and arrange as lattice top. Cook on HI (max. power) for 10 minutes, or until apples are fork-tender.
4. While pie is cooking, preheat conventional oven to 450°. When apples are tender, bake pie in conventional oven for 10 minutes, or until crust is golden brown. Serve warm or cold.

Pecan Pie

6 to 8 servings

1 unbaked 9-inch pastry shell
¼ cup butter or margarine
⅓ cup brown sugar
1 cup dark corn syrup
3 eggs, slightly beaten

1½ teaspoons all-purpose flour
1 teaspoon vanilla extract
⅛ teaspoon salt
1 cup pecan halves

1. Cook pastry shell according to directions above. Set aside.

2. Put butter in microproof mixing bowl. Cook on HI (max. power) for 1 minute, or until melted.
3. Add remaining ingredients. Mix well. Pour mixture into prepared pastry shell. Cook on 50 (simmer) for 25 minutes, or until almost set in center. Cool before serving.

Yogurt Pumpkin Pie

6 servings

¼ cup butter or margarine
1 cup graham cracker crumbs
2 tablespoons sugar
1 cup canned or cooked pumpkin
¼ cup brown sugar, firmly packed
1 teaspoon cinnamon

½ teaspoon nutmeg
¼ teaspoon ginger
¼ teaspoon salt
1 carton (9 ounces) frozen whipped topping
1 carton (8 ounces) vanilla yogurt

1. Put butter in 9-inch glass pie plate. Cook on HI (max. power) for 45 to 60 seconds, or until melted. Add crumbs and sugar; mix.
2. Press mixture into sides and bottom of pie plate. Cook on HI (max. power) for 1½ to 2 minutes, or until heated. Rotate dish once during cooking time.
3. Put pumpkin, brown sugar, cinnamon, nutmeg, ginger, and salt into a large microproof bowl. Combine and cook on HI (max. power) for 1½ to 2 minutes, or until mixture begins to boil. Cool 10 minutes.
4. Remove cover from frozen whipped topping and cook on 30 (defrost) for 1 minute, or until it begins to thaw. Stir carefully.
5. Fold thawed topping and yogurt into cooled pumpkin mixture. Spoon into crust. Refrigerate about 4 hours, or until set.

CAKES, COOKIES, CANDIES

A cake in ten minutes? Yes! When you cook your first cake in your microwave oven, you will be amazed at the speed. It also produces a delectable cake, superior in texture, taste, and height to conventional cooking. Bar cookies are another fast and delicious product. If you've never tried homemade candies before, now's the time. They are especially easy and it's hard to fail when making them in a microwave oven.

ADAPTING YOUR OWN RECIPES

How easy can it be! You're sure to find a recipe here like the one you want to try. And the nicest thing of all is that good old friend, the toothpick. Science has yet to replace it as the most reliable test for doneness. But cakes aren't the only product which promises outstanding success. When you study the candy recipes and note their ease, there's a good chance you will be scurrying for that special magazine issue with homemade candy recipes. Here are our tips on this dessert category:

- Bar cookies work best. Greasing or lining of the microproof baking dish is optional.
- If insufficient browning disturbs you, frost, glaze, or add food coloring to white or yellow batters.
- A serviceable microproof cookie sheet can be made by covering cardboard with waxed paper.
- Round glass baking dishes, and fluted or smooth microproof ring molds work best for cakes. You can make a microproof ring mold of your own by placing a medium-size glass in the center of a round glass baking dish.
- Because your cakes will rise higher in microwave cooking, never fill microproof cake pans more than half full.
- Reduce baking powder and soda by approximately one-fourth when converting a conventional recipe.

USING THE BAKING GUIDE

1. Prepare batter according to recipe or package directions.
2. If cake is to be turned out of dish, line bottom of dish with waxed paper.
3. Bake layers one at a time.
4. Test cakes for doneness with toothpick (inserted in center, it should come out clean if cake is done).

COOKING GUIDE—BAKERY

Cake or Bread	Microproof Container	First Setting and Minutes to Cook	Second Setting and Minutes to cook
Cake mix: 17 to 18½-ounce package, one layer at a time	9-inch round	60 (bake), 7	HI (max. power), 1
Snacking cake mix	8- or 9-inch round	50 (simmer), 8	HI (max. power), 1 to 3
Pound cake: 14-ounce package	9- x 5-inch loaf pan	50 (simmer), 9	HI (max. power), 3 to 5

COOKING GUIDE—BAKERY

Cake or Bread	Microproof Container	First Setting and Minutes to Cook	Second Setting and Minutes to cook
Pineapple upside-down cake mix: 21.5 ounce package	9-inch round	50 (simmer), 7	HI (max. power), 2 to 4
Coffeecake mix	9-inch round	50 (simmer), 7	HI (max. power), 5 to 6
Cupcakes:	Paper cupcake liners in microproof custard cups or microproof muffin tray. Fill one-half full.	50 (simmer),	HI (max. power),
2 cupcakes		1 minute	15 to 30 seconds
4 cupcakes		3 minutes	30 to 45 seconds
6 cupcakes		4 minutes	1 to 1½
Blueberry muffin mix:	Paper cupcake liners in microproof custard cups or microproof muffin tray. Fill one-half full.	50 (simmer),	HI (max. power),
4 muffins		2	1 to 1½
6 muffins		2	1 to 1½
Corn muffin mix:	Paper cupcake liners in microproof custard cups or microproof muffin tray. Fill one-half full.	50 (simmer),	HI (max. power),
4 muffins		4	45 to 60 seconds
6 muffins		4	1 to 1½
Gingerbread mix	8-inch round	50 (simmer), 7	HI (max. power), 2 to 4
Nut bread mix	9- x 5-inch loaf pan	50 (simmer), 9	HI (max. power), 3 to 4

COOKING/DEFROSTING GUIDE—CONVENIENCE BAKERY

Product and Size	Container	Setting and Time	Special Notes
Sweet rolls, coffeecakes, muffins, room temperature	Paper plate, towel, or napkin	80 (reheat)	Add 5 seconds if frozen.
1		10 to 15 seconds	
2		20 to 25 seconds	
4		35 to 40 seconds	
6		45 to 50 seconds	
Whole coffeecake:		80 (reheat)	
room temperature		1 to 1½ minutes	
frozen		1½ to 2 minutes	
French bread, 1 pound:		80 (reheat)	
room temperature		25 to 35 seconds	
frozen		1½ to 2 minutes	
Cakes			
12 to 17 ounces	paper plate, towel, or napkin	30 (defrost), 2 to 3 minutes	Remove from paper carton before defrosting. Let stand 5 minutes.

COOKING/DEFROSTING GUIDE—CONVENIENCE BAKERY

Product and Size	Container	Setting and Time	Special Notes
Cookies			
Brownies or bar cookies, 12 or 13 ounces	Original tray, remove lid	30 (defrost), 2 to 3 minutes	Center pan in oven so pan does not touch sides of oven.
Cookies frozen, cooked	Paper plate, towel, or napkin	30 (defrost)	
1		15 to 20 seconds	
2		30 to 35 seconds	
6		50 to 60 seconds	
Bread			
1 slice, frozen	Paper towel or napkin	30 (defrost), 15 to 20 seconds	
1 loaf, 1 pound	In package	30 (defrost), 2 to 3 minutes	Let stand 3 minutes. Remove metal twist ties before defrosting.
Buns and rolls hot dog, dinner, hamburger	Paper plate, towel, napkin	80 (reheat)	Add 10 seconds if frozen.
room temperature			
1		5 to 10 seconds	
2		10 to 15 seconds	
4		15 to 20 seconds	
6		20 to 25 seconds	

Applesauce Cake

9 servings

¼ cup butter or margarine
1 cup brown sugar, firmly packed
1 cup sweetened applesauce
2 cups all-purpose flour
¾ teaspoon baking soda
1 teaspoon cinnamon

½ teaspoon cloves
½ teaspoon ginger
¼ teaspoon nutmeg
¼ teaspoon salt
½ cup raisins

1. Put butter in large microproof mixing bowl and cook on HI (max. power) for 45 seconds, or until melted.
2. Blend in brown sugar and applesauce. Stir in all remaining ingredients until well blended. Pour into an 8-inch square microproof baking dish, greased on bottom only. Cook on HI (max. power) for 7 minutes.
3. Rotate dish and cook on 60 (bake) for 2 minutes, or until no longer doughy. Cool in pan. When cool, frost with Cream Cheese Frosting (page 148).

Pumpkin Spice Cake

10 to 12 servings

2 eggs
1 cup brown sugar, firmly packed
½ cup sugar
¾ cup cooking oil
1 cup canned pumpkin
1 teaspoon vanilla extract
2 cups all-purpose flour

1 teaspoon salt
½ teaspoon baking powder
½ teaspoon baking soda
½ teaspoon cinnamon
¼ teaspoon nutmeg
¼ teaspoon ginger
¼ cup milk

1. Beat eggs in large mixing bowl; beat in sugars and oil. Stir in pumpkin and vanilla. Stir in all remaining ingredients until smooth.
2. Lightly oil a 12-cup microproof fluted cake mold. Sprinkle with sugar; remove excess. Pour cake batter into prepared mold. Cook on HI (max. power) for 9½ to 10½ minutes, or until toothpick inserted in center comes out clean. Rotate dish once during cooking. Cool 30 minutes before inverting onto serving plate.
3. Cool completely before glazing with Powdered Sugar Glaze (page 148).

If preferred, use 12- x 8-inch microproof baking dish. Grease bottom only. Frost oblong cake with Cream Cheese Frosting (page 148).

Pecan Carrot Cake

10 to 12 servings

4 eggs
1½ cups cooking oil
3 cups carrots cut in 1-inch slices
2 cups sugar, divided
2 teaspoons cinnamon

1 teaspoon salt
1 cup pecans
2 cups sifted all-purpose flour
1½ teaspoons baking powder
1½ teaspoons baking soda

1. Lightly oil 12-cup fluted microproof cake mold. Dust with sugar. Set aside.
2. Put eggs and oil in electric blender container. Blend on high. While blending, add carrots. When carrots reach grated consistency, add 1 cup sugar, cinnamon, salt, and pecans. Blend until pecans are chopped.
3. In large bowl, sift flour, baking powder, baking soda, and remaining sugar. Add blender ingredients. Stir. Pour into prepared cake mold and cook on 50 (simmer) for 15 minutes. Rotate dish one-quarter turn at 3 to 4 minute intervals during cooking time.
4. Cook on HI (max. power) for 4 minutes. Rotate dish one-quarter turn. Cook on HI (max. power) for 4 to 5 minutes, or until cake tests done with toothpick.
5. Let stand 10 minutes. Invert on cooling rack or serving plate. Cool completely. Drizzle on Powdered Sugar Glaze (page 148).

A blender is not necessary, though it is handy, in preparing this recipe. To prepare without a blender, grate carrots first. If carrots are grated, 2 cups are needed. Chop pecans before adding and beat batter well.

Devil's Food Cake

8 to 10 servings

2 cups sifted all-purpose flour
1¼ teaspoons baking soda
¼ teaspoon salt
½ cup shortening
2 cups sugar

½ cup cocoa
1 teaspoon vanilla extract
½ cup buttermilk
2 eggs, beaten

1. Grease bottoms of two 8-inch round microproof cake pans. Line bottoms with waxed paper cut to size. Set aside.
2. In large bowl, sift together flour, baking soda, and salt. Set aside. In separate large bowl, cream shortening, sugar, cocoa, and vanilla until light and fluffy.
3. Put 1 cup water in 2-cup glass measure. Cook on HI (max. power) for 2½ minutes, or until water boils. Stir water, buttermilk, and eggs into creamed mixture. Beat well. Add all dry ingredients and beat until smooth.
4. Pour batter equally into prepared cake pans. Cook, one pan at a time, on 50 (simmer) for 8 minutes.
5. Rotate pan one-quarter turn. Cook on HI (max. power) for 1 to 2 minutes, or until toothpick inserted in center comes out clean.
6. Remove from oven. Let stand 5 minutes. Invert onto cooling rack. Remove waxed paper. Let cool thoroughly before frosting.

For frosting, try Cream Cheese Frosting (page 148) between layers and Chocolate Fudge Frosting (page 149) for the outside. Or use Snow White Frosting (page 149) for the outside. Interesting!

Pineapple Upside-Down Cake

6 servings

3 tablespoons butter or margarine
½ cup brown sugar, firmly packed
1 can (8¼ ounces) sliced pineapple

6 to 10 maraschino cherries, drained
1 package (9 ounces) yellow cake mix
Whipped cream

1. Put butter and sugar in 8-inch round microproof baking dish. Cook on 50 (simmer) for 2 minutes, or until butter is melted. Stir and spread evenly in bottom of dish.
2. Drain pineapple and reserve juice. Arrange pineapple slices atop brown sugar and butter mixture. Dot with cherries.
3. Prepare packaged cake mix according to directions on page 142, reducing required liquid by one tablespoon. Substitute ⅓ cup pineapple juice for part of liquid. Pour batter carefully into baking dish.
4. Cook on 50 (simmer) for 4 minutes. Rotate dish one-quarter turn. Cook on 50 (simmer) for 3 minutes. Rotate dish one-quarter turn again. Cook on HI (max. power) for 1 to 2 minutes, or until toothpick inserted in center comes out clean.
5. Cool for 5 minutes. Invert onto serving plate. Serve warm or cold, topped with whipped cream.

Festive German Chocolate Cake

(Illustrated on page 150)

12 to 14 servings

1 bar (4 ounces) German sweet chocolate	½ teaspoon cloves
1 cup instant mashed potato flakes	½ teaspoon ginger
1½ cups sugar	½ teaspoon salt
1½ cups all-purpose flour	½ cup butter or margarine
1½ teaspoons baking soda	½ cup dairy sour cream
1 teaspoon cinnamon	4 eggs
½ teaspoon nutmeg	½ cup chopped maraschino cherries

1. Break chocolate into large microproof mixing bowl. Add 1 cup water and cook on HI (max. power) for 2 minutes, or until chocolate is melted.
2. Stir until smooth. Stir in potatoes. Add all remaining ingredients except cherries. Mix with electric mixer on low until moistened and then on medium for 3 minutes. Scrape bowl occasionally. Fold in cherries.
3. Generously grease a 12-cup fluted microproof cake mold. Sprinkle with sugar; remove excess. Pour batter into cake mold. Cook on HI (max. power) for 12 to 14 minutes, or until toothpick inserted in center comes out clean. Rotate dish twice during cooking.
4. Cool 30 minutes before inverting onto a cooling rack. Cool completely before frosting.

This cake gains its festive quality from an easy Powdered Sugar Glaze, spooned over the cake and allowed to drizzle down the side.

Powdered Sugar Glaze *(Illustrated on page 150)*

½ cup

1 tablespoon butter or margarine	1½ to 2 tablespoons milk
1 cup powdered sugar	⅛ teaspoon salt
½ teaspoon vanilla extract	

1. Put butter in 2-cup glass measure. Cook on HI (max. power) for 30 seconds, or until melted. Add all ingredients. Start with 1½ tablespoons milk. Add more only if needed to get glaze consistency.
2. Drizzle over cool cake.

Cream Cheese Frosting

1½ cups

1 package (3 ounces) cream cheese	½ teaspoon vanilla extract
2 tablespoons butter or margarine	1 to 2 teaspoons milk
2 cups powdered sugar	

1. Put cream cheese and butter in small microproof mixing bowl. Cook on HI (max. power) for 30 to 45 seconds until softened.
2. Beat in sugar, vanilla, and enough milk to make spreading consistency.

Chocolate Fudge Frosting
1 cup

1 square (1 ounce) baking chocolate
1 cup sugar
⅓ cup milk
¼ cup butter or margarine

⅛ teaspoon salt
1 teaspoon vanilla extract
¼ cup chopped nuts

1. Put chocolate, sugar, milk, butter, and salt in 4-cup glass measure or microproof mixing bowl and cook on HI (max. power) for 2 to 2½ minutes, or until chocolate is melted.
2. Stir to mix. Cook on HI (max. power) for 1½ minutes. Stir after 1 minute.
3. Add vanilla and beat with electric mixer until frosting is almost cool. Add nuts and beat until spreading consistency.

This is sufficient to frost two 9-inch cake layers or a 11- x 7-inch cake.

Snow White Frosting
1½ to 2 cups

1 cup sugar
¼ teaspoon cream of tartar
Dash salt

2 egg whites
1 teaspoon vanilla extract

1. Combine sugar, ½ cup water, cream of tartar, and salt in a 2-cup glass measure. Cook on 70 (roast) for 4 to 5 minutes, or until mixture boils. (200° on candy thermometer.)
2. In small mixing bowl, beat egg whites with electric mixer until soft peaks form. Gradually add hot syrup to egg whites, beating continuously. Continue beating for 5 minutes, or until frosting is thick and fluffy. While beating, add vanilla.

Provides enough frosting for two 9-inch layers or one 13- x 9-inch cake.

Mints *(Illustrated on page 150)*
48 pieces

3 tablespoons butter or margarine
3 tablespoons milk
1 package (15 ounces) creamy white frosting mix

Food coloring (red or green)
½ teaspoon peppermint extract

1. Put butter and milk in 2-quart microproof bowl. Cook on HI (max. power) for 45 seconds, or until butter is melted.
2. Stir in frosting mix. Cook on HI (max. power) for 1½ to 2 minutes, or until bubbly. Stir twice during cooking time. Stir in food coloring to tint. Add extract. Drop mixture by teaspoonfuls onto waxed paper. When cool, store in airtight container.

Almond Bark

1½ pounds

1 cup whole blanched almonds
1 teaspoon butter or margarine

1 pound white chocolate

1. Put almonds and butter in a 9-inch microproof pie plate. Cook on HI (max. power) for 4 to 5½ minutes, or until toasted. Stir twice during cooking. Set aside.
2. Put white chocolate in large microproof mixing bowl and cook on HI (max. power) for 2½ to 3 minutes, or until softened. Stir in almonds and pour onto waxed paper lined baking sheets. Spread to desired thickness and refrigerate until set.

Peanut Brittle

1¼ pounds

1½ cups sugar
½ cup corn syrup
Dash salt
2 cups raw peanuts

1 tablespoon butter or margarine
1 teaspoon baking soda
1 teaspoon vanilla extract

1. Put sugar, corn syrup, ½ cup water, salt, and peanuts in 2-quart microproof bowl or casserole. Cook on HI (max. power) for 5 minutes; stir.
2. Cook on HI (max. power) for 13 to 15 minutes, or until the syrup separates into threads. This is the hard crack stage or 300° on a candy thermometer. Check temperature with thermometer several times during the last few minutes. (Do not leave thermometer in oven while cooking.)
3. Stir in butter, soda, and vanilla just until light and bubbly. Pour onto buttered cookie sheet. Spread. Cool and break into pieces.

You can use dark or light corn syrup. Obviously, the color of your peanut brittle will differ but both are equally delicious.

Rich Chocolate Fudge

48 pieces

4 cups sugar
1 can (14 ounces) evaporated milk
1 cup butter or margarine
1 package (12 ounces) semi-sweet chocolate bits

1 jar (7 ounces) marshmallow creme
1 teaspoon vanilla extract
1 cup chopped nuts

1. In 4-quart microproof bowl, mix sugar, milk, and butter. Cook on HI (max. power) for 20 to 22 minutes, or until a few drops of mixture in cold water forms a soft ball. (234° on candy thermometer. Do not leave thermometer in oven while cooking.) Stir well every 5 minutes during cooking.
2. Stir in chocolate bits and marshmallow creme. Stir until well blended. Add vanilla and nuts; mix. Pour into buttered 9-inch square dish for thick pieces or 7½- x 12-inch dish for thinner pieces. Cool and cut into squares.

Festive German Chocolate Cake with *Powdered Sugar Glaze*
(recipes, p. 148), *Mints* (recipe, p. 149), *Almond Bark,*
Peanut Brittle, Rich Chocolate Fudge

Divinity

2 cups sugar
⅓ cup light corn syrup
2 egg whites

1 teaspoon vanilla extract
½ cup chopped nuts

1. Combine sugar, corn syrup, and ½ cup water in 4-cup glass measure. Cook on HI (max. power) for 3 minutes. Stir thoroughly.
2. Cook on HI (max. power) for 6 to 8 minutes, or until a small amount of syrup dropped in cold water forms a hard ball. (250° on candy thermometer. Do not leave thermometer in oven while cooking.)
3. While syrup is cooking, beat egg whites in a large bowl with electric mixer until stiff peaks form.
4. When syrup is ready, pour in a very thin, slow stream into egg whites. Beat constantly with mixer on high. Add vanilla and beat 6 to 8 minutes, or until mixture is stiff and loses its shine. Fold in nuts and drop mixture by teaspoonfuls on waxed paper. When cool, store in airtight container.

Just for fun, or to carry out a color scheme, you can tint the mixture. Add food coloring with the vanilla in Step 4.

Raisin Spice Drops

½ cup butter or margarine
1 cup brown sugar, firmly packed
1 egg, beaten
¼ cup cold coffee or milk
2½ cups all-purpose flour
½ teaspoon baking soda

½ teaspoon salt
1 teaspoon cinnamon
½ teaspoon nutmeg
½ cup raisins
½ cup chopped nuts

1. Put butter in microproof mixing bowl. Cook on 70 (roast) for 45 seconds, or until melted.
2. Add sugar, egg, and coffee to butter. Blend well. Add all remaining ingredients. Mix.
3. Take piece of cardboard, approximately 11 x 14 inches. Cover with waxed paper. Drop 16 rounded teaspoons of batter on waxed paper. Cook on HI (max. power) for 2½ to 3 minutes, or until cookies are done. Rotate cardboard one-half turn during cooking time. Remove cookies to cooling rack. Repeat with remaining batter.

If you don't care to make a complete batch at one time, cover remaining batter and store in refrigerator up to one week.

Raisin Applesauce Squares

16 squares

¼ cup butter or margarine
⅓ cup sugar
⅓ cup brown sugar, firmly packed
¼ cup applesauce
1 cup all-purpose flour
1 teaspoon baking powder
¼ teaspoon cinnamon

1 egg
1 teaspoon vanilla extract
¼ cup chopped nuts
¼ cup raisins
Topping:
1 teaspoon sugar
1 teaspoon cinnamon

1. Put butter in small microproof mixing bowl. Cook on HI (max. power) for 1 minute.
2. Stir in sugars and applesauce. Add flour, baking powder, and cinnamon. Beat in egg. Stir in vanilla, nuts, and raisins. Spread batter in an 8-inch square microproof baking dish. Cook on HI (max. power) for 4 minutes. Rotate dish one quarter turn twice during cooking.
3. Cook on 50 (simmer) for 2 minutes, or until toothpick inserted in center comes out clean.
4. Remove from oven and sprinkle with mixture of topping ingredients. Cool thoroughly and cut into squares.

Coconut Squares

16 to 20 squares

¼ cup butter or margarine
1 cup graham cracker crumbs
1 teaspoon sugar
1 cup flaked coconut

⅔ cup sweetened condensed milk
½ cup chopped nuts
1 cup semi-sweet chocolate bits

1. Put butter in 8-inch square microproof baking dish. Cook on HI (max. power) for 1 minute, or until melted.
2. Stir in crumbs and sugar; mix. Pat mixture firmly and evenly in bottom of dish. Cook on HI (max. power) for 2 minutes. Cool partially.
3. Mix coconut, milk, and nuts. Spoon carefully over graham cracker crust. Cook on HI (max. power) for 3 minutes. Rotate dish one-half turn once during cooking.
4. Sprinkle with chocolate bits. Cook on HI (max. power) for 1 minute. Spread melted chocolate evenly over coconut mixture. Cool and cut into squares.

Chocolate Chip Bars

32 bars

1 cup butter or margarine
1 cup brown sugar, firmly packed
2 eggs
1 teaspoon vanilla extract
1 cup all-purpose flour

1 cup quick-cooking oatmeal
1 teaspoon baking powder
¼ teaspoon salt
1 cup semi-sweet chocolate bits
¼ cup chopped nuts

1. Put butter in glass microproof mixing bowl. Cook on HI (max. power) for 45 seconds to soften. Beat in remaining ingredients except chocolate and nuts.
2. Spread batter in buttered 12- x 8-inch microproof baking dish. Sprinkle with chocolate and nuts. Cook on 50 (simmer) for 16 to 17 minutes, or until no longer doughy. Rotate dish once during cooking.
3. Cool and cut into squares.

Sour Cream Coffee Cake

9 servings

¼ cup butter or margarine
½ cup sugar
2 eggs
½ teaspoon vanilla extract
1½ cups all-purpose flour
½ teaspoon baking soda
½ teaspoon baking powder
½ cup dairy sour cream

Topping:
⅓ cup brown sugar, firmly packed
2 tablespoons all-purpose flour
½ cup chopped nuts
¼ teaspoon cinnamon
⅛ teaspoon salt
2 tablespoons butter or margarine

1. Cream butter and sugar. Add eggs and vanilla; mix well. Sift together flour, soda, and baking powder. Add to creamed mixture with sour cream. Set aside. Mix topping ingredients until crumbly.
2. Spread half of batter in 8-inch microproof cake dish. Sprinkle half of topping mix over batter. Carefully spread remaining batter and sprinkle with all remaining topping. Cook on 60 (bake) for 4 minutes. Rotate dish one-quarter turn twice during cooking.
4. Cook on HI (max. power) for 4 minutes, or until toothpick inserted in center comes out clean. Let stand 3 minutes before seving. Serve coffee cake warm.

Sticky Buns *(Illustrated on page 87)*

6 servings

⅓ cup firmly packed dark brown sugar
3 tablespoons butter or margarine

⅓ chopped nuts
1 can (8 ounces) refrigerated biscuits

1. Combine brown sugar, butter, and 1 tablespoon water in an 8-inch round microproof baking dish. Cook, uncovered, on 70 (roast) for 2 minutes, or until butter melts.
2. Stir mixture and spread over bottom of pan. Sprinkle nuts over top. Place biscuits on top of mixture. Bake, uncovered, on 70 (roast) for 4 to 5 minutes, or until biscuits are firm and no longer doughy.
3. Let stand about 2 minutes. Invert onto a flat serving plate.

THE WHOLE MEAL METHOD

Dinner is in the oven! It's a familiar saying and we all know what it means. Now you can prepare a whole two- or three-dish meal in your microwave oven and cook it all together. With your experience so far, you know how different the cooking rates of food can be. One way to adjust for this is to start foods which require longer cooking times earlier; those with shorter times later, or just before serving. Seven tested meals are presented here to help you in developing your own Whole Meal menus. If you want to use a recipe in this section separate from the Whole Meal procedure, remove the middle rack and follow the recipe.

ADAPTING YOUR OWN MEALS

Cooking an entire meal requires planning, but it won't be difficult if you remember timing, placement, and cooking sequence. Start with one or more of the simple menu combinations presented in this chapter. You will soon be figuring it out on your own. Some useful hints and tips:

- If all foods take less than 15 minutes individually, add cooking times together and program the menu for the total time.
- If all foods take 15 to 35 minutes individually, add cooking times together and subtract about 5 minutes.
- If any one food takes over 35 minutes, all the food can be cooked in the time suggested for food taking the longest time.
- HI (max. power) is used for all Whole Meal cooking. (Different settings are used when recipes are used separate from Whole Meal method.)
- Whenever the middle rack is not in use, it is removed from the oven.
- When the middle rack is in position, foods cooked on the rack receive more microwave energy than those cooked on the bottom shelf. As a result, foods needing the longest cooking times are placed on the rack.
- The ideal procedure for the Whole Meal features two foods which fit on the middle rack and cook with similar times and one shorter-cooking food for the lower shelf.
- If all foods require the same cooking time, reverse oven location of dishes halfway through cooking period.
- Some foods, such as baked bread, heat so quickly they are added just before the other foods are finished.
- While the middle rack can be used in two positions, the upper position is generally best. Use the lower position whenever you need greater capacity on top. This limits, of course, the height of the dish used on the bottom shelf.

BREAKFAST AT WILLIAMSBURG

Serves 4 to 6

GRAPEFRUIT HALVES
SWEET ROLLS
BACON
SCRAMBLED EGGS
COFFEE

2 to 3 grapefruits
6 eggs
⅓ cup milk
2 tablespoons butter, melted
6 slices bacon
6 bakery sweet rolls
  Coffee

1. Halve, seed, and chill grapefruits. Beat eggs, milk, and butter in 1-quart microproof casserole. Cover. Set aside.
2. Cover microproof dish with 2 layers of paper towels. Put bacon strips on paper towels. Cover with 1 piece of paper towel.
3. Put eggs and bacon in oven as shown in "A". Cook on HI (max. power) for 8 minutes. Serve grapefruit.
4. Stir eggs. Line microproof plate with paper towel. Put sweet rolls on plate. Cover rolls with paper towel. Place dishes as shown in "B". Cook on HI (max. power) for 2 minutes.
5. Remove eggs, bacon, and rolls from oven. Stir eggs; let stand 3 minutes before serving. Serve with coffee.

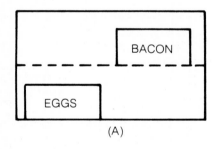

(A)

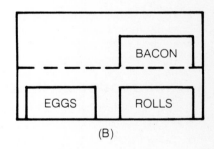

(B)

SAN ANTONIO LUNCHEON
Serves 3

CORN CHIPS
AVOCADO PICANTE SALAD
CHILI
CORN MUFFINS
APPLE CRISP (below)

2 ripe avocados, peeled and pitted
1 jar (8 ounces) Mexican sauce
  Ingredients for Apple Crisp
1 can (24 ounces) chili
1 package (9 ounces) corn chips
3 bakery corn muffins

1. Place avocado halves on salad plates. Fill centers with sauce. Chill.
2. Combine Apple Crisp ingredients in 8-inch square microproof baking dish. Cover with waxed paper. Set aside.
3. Empty chili into 1½-quart microproof casserole. Cover with plastic wrap. Set aside. Wrap corn muffins in paper towel.
4. Place chili and Apple Crisp dishes in oven at position "A". Cook, covered, on HI (max. power) for 5 minutes.
5. Stir chili. Move dishes to position "B". Cook, covered, on HI (max. power) for 3½ minutes. Place corn chips around avocado halves and serve salad.
6. Stir chili. Place muffins in oven. Arrange foods in position "C". Cook, covered, on HI (max. power) for 1½ minutes. Remove all dishes from oven. Serve chili and muffins. Allow Apple Crisp to stand before serving.

(Allow Apple Crisp to stand before serving.)

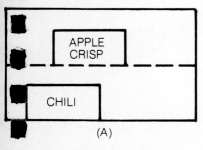

(A)

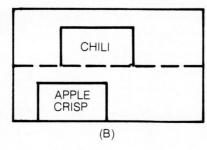

(B)

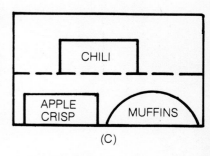

(C)

Apple Crisp
4 servings

4 cups apple slices
½ cup rolled oats
¼ cup all-purpose flour
¼ cup brown sugar

⅛ teaspoon nutmeg
½ teaspoon cinnamon
¼ cup butter or margarine
1 teaspoon lemon juice

1. Put apples in 8-inch square microproof baking dish. Mix remaining ingredients and crumble over top of apples. Cover with waxed paper and cook on HI (max. power) for 8 to 10 minutes. Serve warm or cold.

ALL-AMERICAN CHOP DINNER

Serves 4

TOSSED SALAD
SEASONED PORK CHOPS
PARSLEY POTATOES
MIXED VEGETABLES

4 pork chops
1 envelope (2¼ ounces) coating mix
3 medium potatoes
1 can (16 ounces) mixed vegetables
   Butter
1 tablespoon chopped parsley

1. Shake pork chops in coating mix. Place in 11- x 7-inch glass baking dish. Cover with waxed paper. Set aside.
2. Pare potatoes. Cut into ¾-inch cubes. Put into 8- x 5-inch microproof loaf dish with ¼ cup water. Cover with plastic wrap. Set aside.
3. Drain vegetables. Put into 1-quart microproof casserole. Cover with plastic wrap.
4. Place dishes in oven as shown in "A". Cook, covered, on HI (max. power) for 20 minutes.
5. Stir potatoes. Stir vegetables. Cook, covered, on HI (max. power) for 4 minutes.
6. Check pork. Cook on HI (max. power) for 2 minutes.
7. Remove dishes from oven. Stir vegetables. Dot potatoes with butter. Sprinkle with parsley.

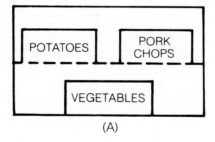

(A)

SUNDAY'S CHICKEN DINNER

Serves 6

TOSSED GREEN SALAD
CHICKEN STEW WITH RAISIN DUMPLINGS (p. 161)
RUBY PEARS (p. 161)

1. Assemble ingredients as required for individual recipes. (Follow your personal favorite for salad.)
2. In 4-quart microproof casserole, combine chicken, celery, onion, bay leaf, peppercorns, salt, bouillon, and 3 cups water. Cover and cook on HI (max. power) for 25 minutes. Stir halfway through cooking time.
3. Put rack in oven. Meanwhile, prepare pears according to steps 1 and 2 of recipe. Add carrots to stew. Combine ¼ cup flour and ½ cup water. Add to stew. Mix.
4. Cover dishes with plastic wrap and place in position "A". Cook on HI (max. power) for 14 minutes.
5. Prepare dumplings for stew according to step 3 of recipe. Remove peppercorns, bay leaf, and chicken bones and skin from stew. Add dumplings to stew. Baste and turn pears. With dishes in position "A", cook, covered, on HI (max. power) for 16 minutes. During this cooking period, prepare and serve salad.
6. Serve stew and dumplings. At dessert time, top pears with whipped cream and serve.

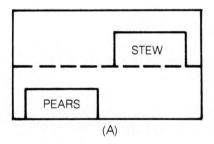

(A)

Chicken Stew with Raisin Dumplings

8 servings

3 pounds frying chicken, cut up
2 stalks celery, cut in 1-inch pieces
1 medium onion, sliced thin
1 bay leaf
4 peppercorns
1 tablespoon salt
3 cubes chicken bouillon
4 cups sliced carrots
¼ cup all-purpose flour

Dumplings:
1½ cups all-purpose flour
2 teaspoons baking powder
1 teaspoon minced parsley
½ teaspoon salt
⅛ teaspoon nutmeg
½ cup raisins
⅔ cup milk
1 egg, slightly beaten
2 tablespoons cooking oil

1. In 4-quart microproof casserole, combine chicken, celery, onion, bay leaf, peppercorns, salt, bouillon, and 3 cups water. Cover and cook on HI (max. power) for 25 minutes. Stir halfway through cooking time.
2. Add carrots. Combine ¼ cup flour and ½ cup water. Add to stew mixture. Stir. Cover and cook on HI (max. power) for 8 minutes.
3. Make dumplings: mix flour, baking powder, and seasonings. Add raisins, milk, egg, and oil. Stir.
4. Remove peppercorns, bay leaf, and chicken bones and skin from casserole. Spoon dumpling batter over mixture. Cover and cook on HI (max. power) for 6 to 8 minutes, or until dumplings are done.

Ruby Pears

6 servings

6 ripe pears
6 whole cloves
1 cup sugar

½ cup sweet vermouth
½ teaspoon red food coloring
Whipped cream

1. Peel pears, leaving the stems on. Stick 1 whole clove into each pear. Set aside.
2. Combine ¼ cup water with remaining ingredients, except whipped cream, in 1½-quart microproof casserole. Add pears.
3. Cover and cook on HI (max. power) for 6 minutes.
4. Baste and turn pears. Cover and cook on HI (max. power) for 6 to 8 minutes.
5. Serve with whipped cream.

SAVANNAH SUPPER

Serves 6

CLAMATO JUICE COCKTAIL
STUFFED FLOUNDER
BROCCOLI
CHOCOLATE PUDDING CAKE (p. 164)

1 can (46 ounces) tomato and clam juice, chilled
1½ pounds fresh broccoli
 Ingredients for flounder
 Ingredients for cake

1. Assemble ingredients as required for individual recipes.
2. Put onion and butter in 2-quart microproof casserole. Cook, uncovered, on HI (max. power) for 3 minutes, or until onion is transparent.
3. Drain mushrooms; reserve liquid. Drain crabmeat and shred with fork. Add mushrooms, crabmeat, cracker crumbs, parsley, salt, and pepper to cooked onion. Mix. Cut flounder horizontally into ¼-inch slices. Spread stuffing mixture over flounder fillets. Roll fillets. Place seam side down in 8-inch square microproof baking dish. Set aside.
4. Prepare topping: put 2 tablespoons butter in 4-cup glass measure. Cook on HI (max. power) for 30 seconds, or until butter is melted. Stir in flour and salt. Add milk to mushroom liquid to make 1 cup. Combine liquid with sherry. Gradually stir milk/mushroom/sherry mixture into flour mixture. Cook on HI (max. power) for 3 minutes, stirring twice at 1 minute intervals. Pour sauce over flounder. Set aside.
5. Remove tough outer leaves from broccoli. Remove tough woody parts of stems. Cut in 1-inch pieces and place in microproof casserole with ½-cup water. Cover with plastic wrap. Prepare cake batter as directed in Chocolate Pudding Cake recipe. Pour into 8x4 microproof loaf pan. Prepare and add topping as directed in cake recipe.
6. Put rack in oven. Position broccoli, flounder, and cake dishes as shown in "A". Cook on HI (max. power) for 27 minutes. Stir broccoli twice during cooking time.
7. Remove cake and allow to cool. Add cheese, paprika, and parsley to flounder. Check broccoli and remove if done. Continue flounder for 4 minutes. If broccoli is not done, with broccoli and flounder dishes in positions "B," cook on HI (max. power) for 9 minutes. Serve juice cocktail.
8. Remove broccoli and flounder from oven. Serve. At dessert time, spoon pudding cake into sherbet glasses topped with whipped cream and serve.

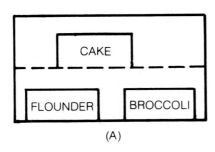

(A)

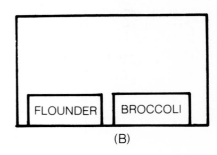

(B)

Stuffed Flounder

6 servings

¼ cup chopped green onion
¼ cup butter
1 can (4 ounces) mushroom pieces
1 can (6½ ounces) crabmeat
½ cup cracker crumbs
2 tablespoons parsley flakes
½ teaspoon salt
¼ teaspoon pepper
2 pounds fresh flounder fillets or any white fish

Topping:
2 tablespoons butter
2 tablespoons all-purpose flour
¼ teaspoon salt
  Milk
⅓ cup sherry
1 cup shredded Cheddar cheese
½ teaspoon paprika
1 teaspoon parsley flakes

1. Put onion and ¼ cup butter in 2-quart microproof casserole. Cook on HI (max. power) for 3 minutes, or until onion is transparent.
2. Drain mushrooms; reserve liquid. Drain crabmeat and shread with fork. Add mushrooms, crabmeat, cracker crumbs, parsley, salt, and pepper to cooked onion. Mix. Cut flounder fillets horizontally into ¼-inch slices. Spread crabmeat stuffing on flounder slices. Roll fish and place, seam side down, in a 12- x 8-inch microproof baking dish. Set aside.
3. Prepare topping: put 2 tablespoons butter in 4-cup glass measure. Cook on HI (max. power) for 30 seconds, or until melted. Stir in flour and salt. Add milk to mushroom liquid to make 1 cup. Combine liquid with sherry. Gradually stir milk/mushroom/sherry liquid into flour mixture. Cook on HI (max. power) for 3 minutes, stirring twice at 1-minute intervals. Pour sauce over flounder.
4. Cook on HI (max. power) for 7 to 8 minutes.
5. Sprinkle cheese, paprika, and parsley over fish. Cook on HI (max. power) for 3 to 4 minutes, or until cheese is melted. Serve.

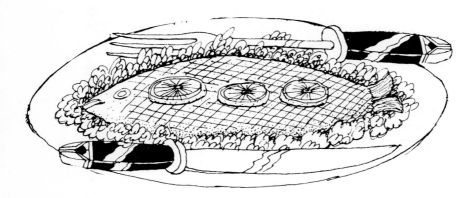

Chocolate Pudding Cake

9 servings

2 tablespoons butter
1 cup all-purpose flour
¾ cup sugar
2 tablespoons cocoa
2 teaspoons baking powder
½ teaspoon salt
½ cup milk

1 teaspoon vanilla extract
½ cup chopped nuts
Whipped cream
Topping:
¾ cup light brown sugar
¼ cup cocoa
1¼ cups water

1. Put butter in 1-cup glass measure. Cook on HI (max. power) for 30 seconds, or until melted.
2. In mixing bowl, sift flour, sugar, cocoa, baking powder, and salt. Stir in milk, butter, vanilla, and nuts. Pour into 8-inch square microproof baking dish.
3. Prepare topping: blend brown sugar, cocoa, and 1¼-cups water in 4-cup glass measure. Pour over batter. Do not stir. Cover with paper towel.
4. Cook on HI (max. power) for 9 to 11 minutes.
5. Remove from oven and let stand 10 minutes. Top with whipped cream and serve.

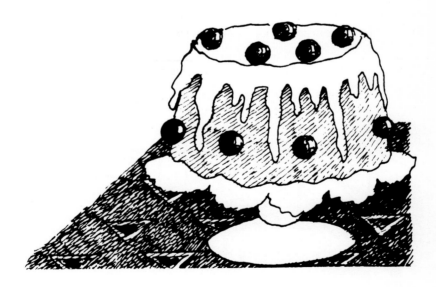

QUICK ITALIAN FIESTA

Serves 4

MELON
BEEF AND SPAGHETTI CASSEROLE
GREEN BEANS ITALIENNE
BAKED APPLE CHUNKS (p. 166)
CAPPUCCINO

1 package (7½ ounces) spaghetti meat-noodle main dish mix
1 pound lean ground beef
1 can (16 ounces) French style green beans
2 tablespoons Italian salad dressing
Ingredients for Baked Apple Chunks
1 ripe melon, chilled
Ingredients for Cappuccino (page 128)

1. Prepare meat-noodle main dish mix according to package directions using ground beef and 4 cups hot water. Put in 2-quart microproof casserole. Cover with plastic wrap. Set aside.
2. Drain beans. Put in 1-quart microproof casserole. Add Italian dressing. Mix. Cover with plastic wrap. Set aside.
3. Prepare Baked Apple Chunks as directed in step 1 of recipe, using an 8- x 5-inch microproof loaf dish. Cover with plastic wrap.
4. Place dishes in oven, positioning as shown in "A". Cook on HI (max. power) for 20 minutes. Meanwhile cut melon in half; remove seeds. Cut in quarters and serve.
5. Stir all three dishes. Cover and cook on HI (max. power) for 5 minutes.
6. Stir all dishes. Cover and let stand for 5 minutes. Serve spaghetti and beans.
7. At dessert time, prepare Cappuccino. Serve with Baked Apple Chunks.

Main dish mixes, whether tuna, hamburger, or another type, are even more convenient with the microwave oven. Follow package directions, then cook on HI (max. power) for 5 minutes. Stir. Cook on 50 (simmer) for 13 minutes.

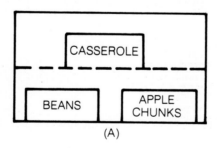

(A)

Baked Apple Chunks

4 servings

4 medium cooking apples	1 teaspoon cinnamon
¼ cup firmly packed brown sugar	2 tablespoons butter or margarine

1. Pare, quarter, and core apples. Put into 1-quart microproof casserole. Combine brown sugar and cinnamon in bowl. Crumble over apples. Dot with butter.
2. Cover and cook on HI (max. power) for 7 to 8 minutes.

COMPANY IS COMING CHINESE DINNER

Serves 8

SPINACH SALAD
SWEET AND SOUR PORK (p. 168)
HOT BUTTERED RICE (p. 168)
GINGERBREAD (p. 168)
HOT LEMON SAUCE (p. 168)
TEA

1. Assemble ingredients as required for individual recipes. (Follow your personal favorite for salad.)
2. Combine carrots and oil in 3-quart (8″ rounded-style) microproof casserole. Cook, covered, on HI (max. power) for 4 minutes.
3. Place rack in oven. Put 2 cups water (for rice) and 1 teaspon salt in 2-quart microproof casserole or 8-x-inch microproof loaf dish. To carrots, add onion, peppers, and pork cubes. Place dishes, angled to fit if handles interfere, in position "A". Cook on HI (max. power) for 11 minutes.
4. Combine ½ cup water with gingerbread mix in 2½-quart microproof bowl. Stir well. Add an additional ½ cup water, stirring slowly. Insert a straight-sided 2-inch-diameter glass, open side up, in center of bowl, forming your own ring-type baking container. (Or use a microproof ring mold.) Set aside.
5. In a bowl, mix ½ cup pineapple syrup and ¼ cup cornstarch. Blend in remaining ingredients of pork recipe. Add to pork mixture, along with pineapple chunks. Stir.
6. Add rice to water. Cover rice and pork casserole with plastic wrap. Place rice, pork, and cake dishes in position "B" and cook on HI (max. power) for 36 minutes.
7. Remove cake and rice. Keep rice covered. Invert cake on serving platter. Set cake and rice aside.
8. Prepare Hot Lemon Sauce by combining sugar, 1 tablespoon cornstarch, and the salt in 2-cup glass measure. Add ¾ cup hot water. Mix. Place pork and sauce dishes in position "C," Cook on HI (max. power) for 3 minutes.
9. Beat egg yolks in 1-quart microproof casserole. Slowly add hot sugar-cornstarch mixture to beaten egg yolks. Using position "C," cook on HI (max. power) for 1 minute or until thickened.
10. Add butter and lemon juice to sauce. Beat until smooth.
11. Dot rice with generous pats of butter. Serve with pork.
12. At dessert time, reheat lemon sauce. Beat first. Cook on HI (max. power) for 2 minutes. Serve with gingerbread and tea.

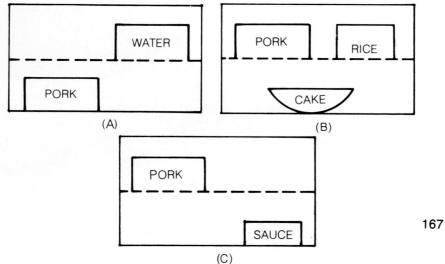

Sweet and Sour Pork

8 servings

4 medium carrots, pared and sliced thin
¼ cup cooking oil
1 medium onion, sliced
2 green peppers, seeded and sliced
2 pounds lean pork, cut in ¾-inch cubes
1 can (16 ounces) pineapple chunks, drained (reserve ½ cup syrup)

¼ cup cornstarch
½ cup soy sauce
½ cup brown sugar
¼ cup vinegar
1 tablespoon Worcestershire sauce
¼ teaspoon hot-pepper sauce
½ teaspoon pepper

1. Put carrots and oil in 3-quart microproof casserole. Stir. Cook, covered, on HI (max. power) for 4 minutes.
2. Add onion, green peppers, and pork. Cover and cook on HI (max. power) for 5 minutes.
3. In a bowl, mix reserved pineapple syrup and cornstarch. Blend in remaining ingredients. Add to pork, along with pineapple chunks. Stir. Cover and cook on HI (max. power) for 10 minutes, or until sauce has thickened and pork is done.
4. Serve with Hot Buttered Rice (below) or chow mein noodels.

Hot Buttered Rice

3 cups

1 teaspoon salt
1 cup long-grain rice

Butter

1. Put 2 cups water and salt in 2-quart microproof casserole. Cook on HI (max. power) for 5 to 6 minutes, or until water boils.
2. Add rice. Cover tightly. Cook on 50 (simmer) for 20 minutes, or until liquid is absorbed.
3. Allow to stand, covered, until rice is tender.
4. Serve dotted with generous pats of butter.

Gingerbread

9 servings

1 package (14 ounces) gingerbread
   mix

1. Combine ½ cup water with gingerbread mix in 2½-quart microproof bowl. Stir well.
2. Add an additional ½ cup water, stirring slowly. Insert straight-sided 2-inch-diameter glass, open side up, in center of bowl, forming your own ring-type baking container. (Or, use microproof ring mold.) Cook on 50 (simmer) for 9 minutes.
3. Rotate bowl one-quarter turn. Cook on HI (max. power) for 2 to 4 minutes, or until toothpick-test confirms doneness.
4. Gently twist glass to remove. Let cake stand 3 to 5 minutes. Invert cake onto serving platter. Serve with Hot Lemon Sauce.

Hot Lemon Sauce

1½ cups

¾ cup sugar
1 tablespoon cornstarch
⅛ teaspoon salt

2 egg yolks
1 tablespoon butter
3 tablespoons lemon juice

1. Put ¾ cup water in 4-cup glass measure. Cook on HI (max. power) for 3 to 4 minutes, or until water boils. Combine sugar, cornstarch, and salt. Add to water. Mix well.
2. Beat egg yolks in microproof bowl. Slowly add hot liquid to beaten egg yolks. Cook on HI (max. power) for 1 minute.
3. Add butter and lemon juice. Beat until smooth.
4. Spoon over cake slices and serve.

Index